WE THE UNICORNS

MY YEAR OF YOUTUBE

You've just taken your first steps to having the best vlogging year. This planner is here to help you feel inspired, get creative and to start making videos.

There are hundreds of ideas across 10 different genres, so there's plenty for you to try, whether you love lifestyle videos, gaming videos or fashion and beauty.

wetheunicorns.com is the voice of the YouTube generation, we live to bring you inside access on your favourite creators, both big and small, plus inspiration, advice and ideas to kick start your own YouTube channel.

So take a deep breath, pick an idea and start creating!

HOW TO USE THIS BOOK

This book is the perfect companion for any aspiring YouTube creator. Part-planner, part-tracker, it's filled with inspirational ideas for videos across 10 different genres so you'll never be stuck for what to make next. Try out the different genres to see which suits you best.

GET INSPIRED

Turn to your favourite genre, or challenge yourself to try something new.

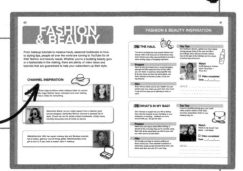

Check out the channel inspiration to discover must-watch YouTubers and then choose which video idea you want to make.

In this section you'll find lots of fun, interesting and sometimes silly ideas plus top tips on how to create your own videos.

Watch the example videos for some inspiration, and then jot down any notes or ideas you have (there's space for more notes at the end of each section). When you've completed the vlog, tick the box and add the date.

You'll notice these different colours on the numbers for each idea. This represents the difficulty of each idea. Start with something easy, or challenge yourself with a medium or difficult video if you're feeling a bit more confident.

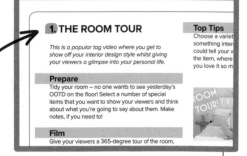

1. THE ROOM TOUR

This is a popular tag video where you get to show off your interior design style whilst giving your viewers a glimpse into your personal life.

Prepare
Tidy your room – no one wants to see yesterday's OOTD on the floor! Select a number of special items that you want to show your viewers and think about what you're going to say about them. Make notes, if you need to!

Film
Give your viewers a 365-degree tour of the room,

Top Tips
Choose a variety something inter could tell your v the item, where you love it so m

 Easy   Medium   Hard

GET THINKING

At the end of each section there's space for you to write 10 video ideas of your own. Get creative – you might even come up with a never-before-seen video!

GET PLANNING

Use the planner pages to plan and script your videos. This is great for videos where you need to stay on topic. You can plan what you want to say and note down any key points you need to cover.

GET ANALYSING

The analytics pages are a great way to keep track of your videos' performances. Add in the statistics of your videos one week after upload and you'll have a great overview of what's working, what's not and who your audience is.

LIFESTYLE

From daily vlog updates and room tours to routines, advice, Q&A and of course Vlogmas, lifestyle videos and vlogs make up some of the most popular content on YouTube. Plus, they're easy to make because they're all about... your life! You can literally start recording now, from your bedroom.

CHANNEL INSPIRATION:

Zoella: Queen of the lifestyle vid, Ms Sugg covers all bases. She's our go-to-girl for monthly faves, chatty advice, day-in-the-life vlogs, silly collabs and general inspiration.

The Michalaks: This completely cute family upload weekly lifestyle vlogs that are almost mini movies. Check them out for real-life videos and take some tips from their sleek editing style.

The Anna Edit: Anna is ruling at the lifestyle game right now, offering advice, style, wellness and fitness vlogs amongst her trademark, on-point beauty tutorials.

LIFESTYLE INSPIRATION

1. THE ROOM TOUR

This is a popular tag video where you get to show off your interior design style whilst giving your viewers a glimpse into your personal life.

Prepare
Tidy your room – no one wants to see yesterday's OOTD on the floor! Select a number of special items that you want to show your viewers and think about what you're going to say about them. Make notes, if you need to!

Film
Give your viewers a 365-degree tour of the room, pointing out anything interesting and then focus in on your special items.

Top Tips
Choose a variety of items that have something interesting about them. You could tell your viewers a funny story behind the item, where you got it from, or just why you love it so much.

Watch
Room Tour! | Meredith Foster – Meredith Foster

☐ **Video completed**

Date ____/____/____

NOTES:..
....
....

2. MONTHLY FAVES

Make this a monthly staple on your channel. It's your opportunity to rave about everything you've been loving in the last month, from products and style items to TV shows, books and anything at all!

Prepare
Throughout the month keep a note of things you want to include in the video. Before you start filming line everything up, make sure it's in easy reach and have a think about what you want to say about each item.

Film
Show the product to your viewers, and talk about why you like it. Make sure to include information about price and where they can get it from too. Pop this info into the description box.

Top Tips
If you're a beauty vlogger, focus on beauty products, if you're a booktuber, talk about books. Keep it focused to keep your viewers interested. But of course, rules can always be broken.

Watch
MONTHLY FAVOURITES – it does what it says on the tin (playlist) – The Anna Edit

☐ **Video completed**

Date ____/____/____

NOTES:..
....
....

LIFESTYLE INSPIRATION

3. 50 FACTS ABOUT ME

This is a fantastic first video idea to help viewers get to know and love the leading star of your YouTube channel – you.

Prepare

Write down 50 fun and interesting facts about yourself. Give viewers the inside scoop on things like your favourite food, music and films, your pets, nicknames, hobbies, weird habits, phobias and anything else that makes you tick.

Film

Talk through your facts in front of the camera, adding extra details where relevant or telling the stories behind them. 50 is a lot of facts to get through however, so keep it snappy to stop viewers getting bored.

Top Tips

It's totally normal to take a while to get fully comfortable chatting in front of the camera. Pretend you're just talking to a close friend instead and you'll soon find your vlogs flow more naturally.

Watch

50 Facts About Me | Zoella – Zoella

☐ **Video completed**

Date ____/____/____

NOTES:..
....
....

4. A DAY IN THE LIFE

Get real and give viewers a sneaky peek into your life by vlogging all the things you get up to during one day. It's basically like your own online video diary.

Prepare

It helps to film this video on a day where you have a lot going on, whether it's a fun trip with friends or a special event. Though it might not exactly represent an average day in your life, it'll be a lot more interesting to watch than a day spent on the sofa.

Film

Show viewers what it's like to be you. If something fun is happening, don't forget to get your camera out and record it. Film more than you need and edit the footage into a montage of the day's highlights.

Top Tips

These videos help your viewers get to know you on a more personal level, but be careful not to get too personal. Don't mention where you go to school or work and keep your address secret.

Watch

A Day In The Life: New York | The Anna Edit – The Anna Edit

☐ **Video completed**

Date ____/____/____

NOTES:..
....
....

LIFESTYLE INSPIRATION

5. THE Q&A

Q&A's are an essential upload for any channel. They help you connect with your subscribers and they're also one of the easiest vlogs to film when you're short on time or all out of ideas.

Prepare
Prepare in advance by letting your viewers know you'll be making a Q&A and asking them to leave any burning questions for you in the comments section. You can also reach out on other social media sites like Twitter and Instagram.

Film
Sit down in front of the camera to answer the questions. Whether they're about your favourite pizza toppings or something more serious, the more thought and honesty you put into your answers the better.

Top Tips
Give recognition to the viewers who asked you the questions by displaying a screenshot of their question and username as you answer each one.

Watch
HONEST Q&A WITH ZOE!! – Mark Ferris

☐ **Video completed**
Date ___/___/___

NOTES:...
....
....

6. DRAW MY LIFE

The ever-popular Draw My Life Tag gives you the chance to share your life story while showing off your artistic abilities.

Prepare
Write an outline of the story you want to tell. Focus on the important parts of your life, from being born up until the present moment. You could talk about your family and friends, events that have had a strong influence on you or lessons you've learned.

Film
Use a whiteboard and pen to sketch out your story. Set up your camera (or ask someone else) to film from above, focusing on your hands as you draw and erase each illustration. Take your time; vloggers usually speed up the drawing process during editing, as well as recording the voiceover.

Top Tips
Don't worry if you're not a whizz at drawing, stick figures work just fine so long as you have a well thought-out story line.

Watch
Draw My Life ♥ Wengie – Wengie

☐ **Video completed**
Date ___/___/___

NOTES:...
....
....

LIFESTYLE INSPIRATION

7. WHAT I GOT FOR...

Complete this video for your birthday

A guaranteed video idea for at least one day that rolls around every year... your birthday! Showing off your pressie stash is the perfect way to celebrate and say thanks to everyone who's spoiled you.

Prepare
Whether it's your birthday presents or Christmas haul, gather all your gifts within easy reach of the camera and make a note of who gave you what.

Film
Show each of your presents to camera, telling viewers who each one was from and why you were happy to receive it.

Top Tips
There's a fine line between showing off your presents and seeming like you're bragging. Remember to say a big thank you to all the people who bought you gifts, and remember not everyone is as lucky as you are.

Watch
What I Got for Christmas 2016!! Alisha Marie – AlishaMarie

☐ **Video completed**

Date ____/_____/_____

NOTES:...

....

....

8. THE BEST FRIEND TAG

What better person to make a video with than your very best pal? Take on the Best Friend Tag and share your friendship with the world.

Prepare
Get a set of questions ready for you and your BFF to answer. There are lots of lists already available on the Internet or you could come up with some of your own.

Film
Make a Q&A style video, taking it in turns to ask each other questions and tell stories about your friendship. Most importantly, just relax and have fun together. The best thing about these videos is getting to see the bond between two friends.

Top Tips
There are other variations of this video to try with all of your nearest and dearest, including The Sibling Tag, The Boyfriend Tag and The Roommate Tag.

Watch
Best Friend Tag | velvetgh0st ♥ – Gabriella ♥

☐ **Video completed**

Date ____/_____/_____

NOTES:...

....

....

LIFESTYLE INSPIRATION

9. MORNING ROUTINE

The most popular of all the routine videos. Make your own to show viewers how you usually like to start your day.

Prepare

Morning routines are a peek into your life beyond the usual setting so make sure everything's tidy. You'll then need to prepare the scene, like setting an alarm to go off, laying out breakfast items and picking the perfect outfit to put on.

Film

Recruit a friend or family member to film you as you go about your usual morning routine, from pretending you've just woken up to stepping out the front door. Once you've edited all the footage you'll need to record a voiceover narrating what you're doing at every step.

Top Tips

Once you've nailed the morning routine you can move onto night routines, school routines... there's literally a routine for every season. Or, if you fancy something a little less perfectly put together, try out a spoof routine too.

Watch

SPRING MORNING ROUTINE 2017!! – MissRemiAshten

☐ **Video completed**

Date ____/____/____

NOTES: ....
....
....

10. DAILY VIDEO

Not for the fainthearted, some vloggers turn their day in the life videos into a full time habit and upload footage every single day.

Prepare

You don't need a fancy camera to become a daily vlogger, since part of the appeal comes from the realness and relatability. However, you will need to come across well on camera, so do practise beforehand by filming yourself and watching the footage back to see where you can improve.

Film

Let viewers into your life by filming your daily antics and turning it into a ten-minute vlog that tells the story of your day. Look directly into the camera and chat to your viewers like you would talk to a friend. Don't forget to film something every day of the week.

Top Tips

Vlogging in public definitely takes time to get used to, but conquer your fears and your vlogs will be much better without huge gaps between 'scenes' whenever you go outside.

Watch

WHAT ARE WE DOING... – PointlessBlogVlogs

☐ **Video completed**

Date ____/____/____

NOTES: ....
....
....

LIFESTYLE INSPIRATION

11. WHAT TO DO...

These videos are full of ideas for fun things to do when you're bored. Make your own and become your viewers' go-to channel for all kinds of life inspiration.

Prepare
Pick a title for your video and use this topic to come up with a list of entertaining things for your viewers to get up to. It could be ideas for things to do during the summer or Christmas holidays, with friends, at the weekend, or just on a lazy day at home.

Film
From painting and DIY projects to a photoshoot with friends, go through your ideas one by one and film yourself acting out the activities.

Top Tips
It's a good idea to upload your video during times of the year when people have a lot of spare time, such as the school holidays. Bored viewers searching for something to do will stumble straight into your video.

Watch
What To Do When You're Bored On Spring Break! I 10 Fun Ideas! – MyLifeAsEva

☐ **Video completed**
Date ___/____/____

NOTES:..
....
....

12. ADVICE

YouTube is often the place people turn to when they need help. If there's an issue you have experience dealing with and you think you can help others, upload a video sharing your advice.

Prepare
Pick a topic close to your heart that you perhaps have personal experience dealing with. Whether it's relationship advice, confidence tips or disclosing how you've dealt with bullies, it's a good idea to draft out what you're going to say before you film and do research if you need to.

Film
Make an honest video talking to your viewers directly to share your own experiences. Whether it's an everyday worry or a more serious issue, try to offer your own words of wisdom, advice and support.

Top Tips
Above all, be genuine and sincere in your video. Viewers are looking to connect with people who have been through the same things they have and understand exactly how they feel.

Watch
How To Deal With Bullying – Marcus Butler

☐ **Video completed**
Date ___/____/____

NOTES:..
....
....

LIFESTYLE INSPIRATION

13. WHAT'S ON MY PHONE?

These videos are an easy way to give viewers a little insight into your life by showing them one of the most important and personal things you own... your phone.

Prepare
You already have the phone, you already have all your apps downloaded... now you just need to show it off. Look through your home screen before filming and think about what you'll say about each of your apps.

Film
Record footage straight from your phone screen as you talk viewers through the things you have on there, from the background picture to your music, any customisations you've made and the apps you use the most.

Top Tips
Be careful not to show any personal information you may keep on your phone and remember to turn off notifications before filming if you don't want everyone to get a peek at your personal messages.

Watch
WHAT'S ON MY IPHONE 7 + TOP 5 BEST APPS! | Aspyn Ovard
– Aspyn Ovard

☐ **Video completed**

Date ____/____/____

NOTES:...
....
....

14. INTERNATIONAL WOMEN'S DAY

Complete this video on March 8th

March 8th is International Women's Day, where we celebrate the achievements of amazing women all over the world. Use this important day to shout-out to all the wonderful women who rock your world.

Prepare
Think about the women who inspire you. It could be your BFF, your mum or even a celeb. Write a list of all the things you admire about them.

Film
Sit down in front of the camera to chat about each of the women you've chosen, your relationship and all the ways they inspire you. Feel free to get a bit cheesy, this is basically a thank you video for the special ladies in your life.

Top Tips
Celebrate girl power and come up with your own ideas for other videos to upload on International Women's Day.

Watch
Who Inspires Me Most? – Sprinkleofglitter

☐ **Video completed**

Date ____/____/____

NOTES:...
....
....

LIFESTYLE INSPIRATION

15. GIFT GUIDES

Take the stress out of Christmas shopping by helping your viewers find the best gifts for their loved ones, from sisters and mothers to dads, besties and brothers.

Prepare
Decide what type of gift guide to make. It could be presents specifically for girls or guys, broken down by family member or budget, or one that encompasses everything. Now get your shop on and put together the perfect gift list.

Film
Whether its budget-friendly finds, stocking fillers or fancier things, go through each of the presents and explain why you picked them. Include links for each item in the description bar to make life (and shopping) easier for your viewers.

Top Tips
Unless you're using the presents in your guide for your own gift giving, you don't necessarily need to go out and buy every item you're talking about. It's all about inspiration, so shop online and show pics from the Internet pages.

Complete this video as part of Vlogmas

Watch
STOCKING FILLER Gifts - 2016! I – Fleur DeForce

☐ **Video completed**

Date ___/___/___

NOTES: ....
....
....

16. THE 'MY FIRST TIME' TAG

Never filmed the First Time Tag? Well, there's a first for everything. This fun YouTube tag is all about the various 'first' experiences in your life.

Prepare
Find a list of the First Time questions, there's loads floating about. It helps to think through your answers beforehand so you don't stumble on camera.

Film
What was your first word? Who was the first YouTuber you subscribed to? When was your first crush? These are the kinds of questions you'll answer in front of the camera when you film the video.

Top Tips
The great thing about this video is that you can pick and choose which questions to answer. For example, you don't have to talk about things like your first crush or kiss, but if you have a hilarious memory you want to share with your subscribers then go ahead.

Watch
FIRST TIME TAG – Emily Canham

☐ **Video completed**

Date ___/___/___

NOTES: ....
....
....

LIFESTYLE INSPIRATION

17. 10 REASONS TO BE HAPPY

Here's a date for your diary – March 20th is International Day of Happiness. Give your viewers something to smile about by uploading a video all about feeling happy.

Prepare
From the simple things like pizza and puppies to great things that are currently going on in the world, come up with a list of 10 things that make you smile.

Film
Use your list to film a chatty video, talking viewers through your 10 reasons. If you yourself are positive and cheery when you film it's bound to put people watching you in a good mood too... happiness is infectious!

Top Tips
To get yourself in the right mood for filming, spend some time on your feet moving and dancing around beforehand. Listening to music can help to loosen you up too.

Complete this video on March 20th

Watch
10 THINGS TO BE HAPPY ABOUT – Andrea Russett

☐ **Video completed**
Date ____/____/____

NOTES:...
....
....

18. CHANNEL TRAILER

Now that you're starting to get some more viewers it's time to make a trailer to introduce potential subscribers to your channel.

Prepare
Before making a video trailer you should have enough uploads under your belt to be able to pick out your best moments. These clips will introduce unsubscribed visitors to your channel and outline the kind of things they can expect to see more of.

Film
Think of the video like a movie trailer. Look through your other videos and pull out the clips that highlight what your channel is all about and why viewers should subscribe. Edit the footage together into a short and snappy introductory video that'll have people hooked.

Top Tips
Make your finished trailer the featured video on your YouTube channel page. That way, new viewers will get to see your best content straight away and are more likely to stick around and subscribe.

Watch
Channel Trailer | Karlie Kloss – Klossy

☐ **Video completed**
Date ____/____/____

NOTES:...
....
....

LIFESTYLE INSPIRATION

19. STORYTIME

Do you have one of those crazy stories that has to be seen to be believed? Well, the Storytime video offers you the perfect platform to tell it...

Prepare
Pick one of your life experiences to talk about – the more interesting and out there the better. From how you met your BFF to strange experiences, horror stories or embarrassing moments, Storytime videos are having a moment.

Film
Break down those barriers, open up and tell a captivating story on camera. These videos help your viewers feel more connected to you on a personal level. Encourage interaction by asking them to share their own experiences in the comments section, and don't forget to reply.

Top Tips
Come up with an interesting title for your video and a thumbnail to match to get viewers to click on your video.

Watch
MY EMBARRASSING CRUSH STORY TIME | JENerationDIY – JENerationDIY

☐ **Video completed**

Date ____/____/____

NOTES:..
....
....

20. GIVEAWAY

YouTubers do giveaway videos to celebrate special milestones on their channel or just as a way of saying a big thank you to subscribers by giving something back.

Prepare
You'll need to have something you're prepared to give away as a prize. This will depend on the size of your channel, but it doesn't need to be anything big. For example, you could do a back to school giveaway to win some cool new school supplies or give away something you made in a DIY video.

Film
Tell your viewers the reason why you've decided to do a giveaway and show the prize to the camera. Let people know how they can enter and when you are going to be picking the winner.

Top Tips
Some vloggers ask viewers to like the video, leave a comment and subscribe in order to enter the giveaway. This is a sure way (if a little sneaky) to grow your channel.

Watch
School Supply Haul + Giveaway! | Maddi Bragg – Maddi Bragg

☐ **Video completed**

Date ____/____/____

NOTES:..
....
....

LIFESTYLE INSPIRATION

21. VLOGMAS

Complete these videos throughout December

The month of December can only mean one thing: it's time to do Vlogmas! Take on this popular vlogging challenge and upload one festive vlog every day in the run up to Christmas.

Prepare
Vlogmas means 24 whole videos of Christmassy content, so it's a very good idea to plan out some video ideas in advance. As well as daily vlogging, other popular ideas for Vlogmas vids include decoration DIYs, baking Christmas goodies, festive makeup tutorials and seasonal shopping hauls.

Film
This is like filming a daily vlog, but much more festive. From decorating the tree to gift giving and going to parties, let viewers in on all the exciting antics you get up to over the Christmas period.

Top Tips
Stick with it! Vlogmas can be a big boost to your channel and is also an excellent way to try out daily vlogging when you have more time to commit to it during the Christmas holidays.

Watch
DECORATING OUR CHRISTMAS TREE | VLOGMAS DAY 2 – Tanya Burr

☐ **Video completed**

Date ___/___/____

NOTES:...
....
....

22. CHILDHOOD CRINGE

Take a stroll down memory lane and invite your viewers to come along for the ride. Upload the ultimate throwback video, looking back on (and cringing at) some of your childhood memories.

Prepare
First you'll need to dig out some of your childhood memorabilia, whether that's old photos, videotapes, memory boxes or possessions. Childhood memories can be especially hilarious – the cringier the better.

Film
You could make a slideshow of old photos and narrate them, go through your old memory boxes on camera, or watch old home videos and film yourself reacting to them.

Top Tips
Your childhood stories and embarrassing memories are totally unique to you, so why not share some during the video? Your viewers will love to laugh along with you.

Watch
Cringing At Old Embarrassing Photos | Zoella – Zoella

☐ **Video completed**

Date ___/___/____

NOTES:...
....
....

LIFESTYLE INSPIRATION

23. FILM A DAY WITH FRIENDS

Whether you're having a cosy sleepover, going shopping or just goofing around, collabs with your friends are loads of fun to film.

Prepare
Make some plans to hang out with your pals. Sharing your fun times with a group of friends in your videos makes viewers feel like they're a part of your friend group too.

Film
Take a camera along on your day out with friends. Film all the fun things that happen and then edit the footage into a highlight reel of your day. Your viewers should feel like they were there along with you.

Top Tips
People you know may not always want to be filmed so make sure you ask your friends for their permission before putting them in a video.

Watch
ROAD TRIP BEGINS – MoreZoella

☐ **Video completed**
Date ___/____/____

NOTES:..
....
....

24. MY NEW YEAR'S RESOLUTIONS

Complete this video for January 1ˢᵗ

This is the ideal video to kick start the New Year on YouTube. Share your New Year's Resolutions with your subscribers – they might actually make you stick to them.

Prepare
Make a list of New Year's Resolutions and goals you want to achieve in the upcoming year. Whether it's starting an interesting hobby or taking steps towards achieving a lifetime ambition, make your video unique by setting your own personalised goals.

Film
Let viewers know what your New Year's goals are, why you want to achieve them and what you plan to do to make it happen. Try to upload your video

on New Year's Day when other people will be looking for New Year's inspiration of their own.

Top Tips
You could make a follow-up video during the year updating your viewers on how you're getting on with your goals.

Watch
My 2017 New Years Resolutions | Shay Mitchell – Shay Mitchell

☐ **Video completed**
Date ___/____/____

NOTES:..
....
....

LIFESTYLE INSPIRATION

25. QUESTIONS NOBODY ASKS TAG

Put a spin on the usual Q&A video by filming the Questions Nobody Asks Tag.

Prepare
Choose your never asked questions from lists on the web; aim to pick around 50 questions. From whether you've got freckles to your perfect cup of tea, there are plenty of questions to choose from.

Film
Film it in the same way as a normal Q&A: sit in front of a camera, have your questions ready and prepare to Q and slay.

Watch
Questions Nobody Asks Tag! | Meredith Foster – Meredith Foster

☐ **Video completed**
Date ____/____/____

26. BACK TO SCHOOL

Videos all about school are big business on YouTube. Make a fun 'back to school' video of your own to ease your viewers back into the school season.

Prepare
There are so many different videos you could choose to make, such as a back to school supplies DIY, advice videos on anything from teachers to exam tips or a new term fashion lookbook.

Film
There are lots of back to school videos already out there, so whatever you decide to film, try to put your own twist on it.

Complete this video at the end of the school holidays

Watch
Back To School: Life Hacks & Easy tips! – Bethany Mota

☐ **Video completed**
Date ____/____/____

27. FURRY FRIENDS

Everyone knows that the people of the Internet are obsessed with pets. If you have a cute animal of your own take full advantage and film a video with it.

Prepare
Decide what kind of pet-based video to make. Perhaps you have some tips on how to take care of an animal, or you simply want to introduce your subscribers to your furry friend.

Film
Point a camera at your dog/cat/hamster/rabbit/bird/ whatever pet you have and hit record.

Watch
Meet My Puppy Harley! ♥ – Amanda Steele

☐ **Video completed**
Date ____/____/____

LIFESTYLE IDEAS

Write 10 of your own ideas for lifestyle videos to film. If you've got a special event coming up, you could film a day-in-the-life or Q&A about it, share an unusual hobby with your fans or invent your own tag.

28 ....
....
....
....

29 ....
....
....
....

30 ....
....
....
....

31 ....
....
....
....

32 ....
....
....
....

33

34

35

36

37

NOTES:

LIFESTYLE NOTES

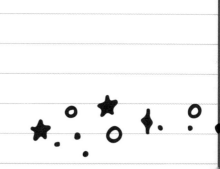

GAMING

Gamers play and share their passion for video games online, and with their fun-packed play alongs, expert tips, reviews and hilarious reactions, it's no wonder that over half of the world's most watched channels are all about gaming. You don't need mega expensive equipment to get going – lots of top gamers started out with only a camera and a computer. Just grab a game and give it a go.

CHANNEL INSPIRATION:

PewDiePie: The undisputed king of YouTube, Pewds is known across the globe for his unfiltered sense of humour, indie video game play alongs and hilariously OTT reactions to the games that he plays.

jacksepticeye: Arguably 'the most energetic video game commentator on YouTube', Jack never fails to entertain viewers with his loud personality while he plays everything from Happy Wheels to GTA.

iHasCupQuake: Tiffany, aka Cupquake, proves that girls can game with the best of them. Alongside her much loved Minecraft Oasis series, she merges crazy app gameplays, creativity and collabs with her husband, friends and fellow gamers.

GAMING INSPIRATION

38. GAMING MONTAGE

Gaming montages are made up of clips of the most enjoyable moments of gameplay footage. This is a great type of video to kick off your gaming channel with since they're fun to watch and fairly easy to make.

Prepare
The first thing you'll need to do is record your gameplay. You can simply set up a camera to point at the screen, but your videos will be much better quality if you can get your hands on a capture card – a device that connects between your console, your TV and your PC, and allows you to capture direct footage in HD.

Film
Just play your favourite game for a few hours and edit the footage down to the very best bits.

Viewers love to see spectacular stunts, fail montages and funny moments.

Top Tips
Aim to play for around one to two hours and cut it down to five minutes of funniness.

Watch
DAN AND PHIL FUNNY GAMING MONTAGE – DanAndPhilGAMES

☐ **Video completed**
Date ____/____/____

NOTES: ....
....
....

39. LET'S PLAY

One of the most popular uploads, Let's Play videos are also a lot of fun to make since you get to record yourself playing all your favourite games.

Prepare
Choose the game carefully – it should either be one that you already know and love, or one that you think will be entertaining for your viewers to watch being played. The more interesting the game is, the better the video will be.

Film
As well as filming the actual gameplay content, you'll need to set up a microphone to record yourself as you narrate your progress through the game and react to what's happening on screen. It's easy to get carried away when you're playing a game, but don't forget to keep talking.

Top Tips
As a smaller YouTuber you'll need to be more brutal during editing to avoid videos being too long and keep viewers' attention. Make use of free editing options like Windows Movie Maker, or iMovie for Macs, which will probably have everything you need in the beginning.

Watch
Let's Play Minecraft (playlist) – RoosterTeeth

☐ **Video completed**
Date ____/____/____

NOTES: ....
....
....

GAMING INSPIRATION

40. WALKTHROUGH

Walkthrough videos help viewers learn how to play or progress through a game, and also offer the perfect chance to show off your gaming skills.

Prepare
Walkthroughs are more instructional than a Let's Play video, so you'll need to pick a game that you have a good knowledge of playing beforehand. It may also help to gather a few notes for the commentary before you start filming.

Film
Guide your viewers through the video game, explaining what you're doing and offering your advice. This could include tips on game strategy, technique, how to complete quests, improve characters, gather materials or defeat opponents.

Top Tips
Your audio commentary is a key part of this video, so make sure viewers can hear you loud and clear. Some gamers use external microphones to get the very best sound quality, but you can also use the built-in microphone on a gaming headset.

Watch
The Walking Dead Survival Instinct Gameplay Walkthrough Part 1 - Intro (Video Game) – theRadBrad

☐ **Video completed**

Date ____/____/____

NOTES:...
....

41. GAMING SERIES

If you think one of your Let's Play or Walkthrough videos is doing well, now could be the perfect time to turn it into a multi-episode gaming series.

Prepare
Whether it's a Minecraft survival series or a complete Call of Duty walkthrough, decide what your gaming series will be and try to plan out a few episodes in advance so you can keep your content focused in each individual video.

Film
Episodes should ideally build off of one another, so it could be a good idea to film more than one video during a long gaming session to keep consistency. Developing a regular series is also a great way to build up a loyal audience and keeps viewers coming back for more.

Top Tips
Create a separate playlist for your gaming series on your main YouTube channel page so that viewers can find it easily.

Watch
UNDERTALE - Part 1 (Full Series) – PewDiePie

☐ **Video completed**

Date ____/____/____

NOTES:...
....
....

GAMING INSPIRATION

42. MINECRAFT

If you're into gaming, and you're not already making Minecraft videos, then you probably should be. More people watch videos about Minecraft than any other game, so unsurprisingly some of the most successful YouTubers are those who specialise in the block-building game.

Prepare
If you don't already have the Minecraft game, you can find the classic version online for free – all you need to do is create an account.

Film
Whether it's focusing on ideas for new things to create, mini games, lucky block challenges, Minecraft comedy, mod showcases or impressive builds, the opportunities for making Minecraft videos are endless.

Top Tips
Be original. With so many Minecraft videos already out there, putting your own unique spin on a video idea will help yours to stand out from the crowd.

Watch
Minecraft Mini-Game : HIDE AND SEEK! – Sky Does Minecraft

☐ **Video completed**
Date ____/____/_____

NOTES:...
....
....

---

43. GAME REVIEW

Just got a new video game that you can't wait to try? Take this chance to make a video telling your viewers all about it.

Prepare
Play the game before making the video so you have time to form an overall opinion on it – make notes or write a script so you don't forget important points. Whether it's good or bad, viewers want informative reviews with honest opinions.

Film
You can simply film yourself talking to camera, but it's also a good idea to insert actual footage of the game as you talk through it. This allows viewers to experience the game for themselves before they decide to buy it.

Top Tips
Keep up-to-date with new video game releases and trends. Lots of people look for reviews after a big game comes out, so the sooner you can get a video up the better chance your video has of being discovered in search.

Watch
Star Wars: Battlefront - Game Review – Chris Stuckmann

☐ **Video completed**
Date ____/____/____

NOTES:...
....
....

GAMING INSPIRATION

44. REACTION

An entertaining and easy-to-make version of the classic review video, make a reaction video to capture your initial impressions and real-time reactions to playing a video game for the first time.

Prepare

You'll need to set up a camera or webcam to focus on your face so that viewers can see and hear your reactions to the game as you play along. This footage can then be edited together onscreen.

Film

In this type of video the viewer's focus is just as much on you as the game content itself. Bear this in mind and try to keep it as entertaining as possible (during filming as well as the edit) – whether you're sharing your first thoughts, jumping with fright or getting thoroughly frustrated.

Top Tips

Make yourself the main attraction by showcasing your own unique personality. Top gamer PewDiePie became famous for his crazy screaming and funny facial reactions.

Watch

[FUNNY] TOP SCARIEST MOMENTS OF GAMING! 100'000 Subs Special! (Episode 6) – PewDiePie

☐ **Video completed**

Date ___/____/____

NOTES:...
....
....

45. IMPOSSIBLE LET'S PLAY CHALLENGE

Amp up the difficulty level of any game by taking part in the Impossible Let's Play challenge. Invented by popular gamer Markiplier, the aim is to endure physical challenges at the same time as playing a game.

Prepare

Whether (like Mark) it might be running on a treadmill while trying to operate in Surgeon Simulator or covering your face in clothes pegs every time you die in Sonic Unfair, you'll first need to choose a game to play and a challenge to complete – the more suffering the better.

Film

A split screen set-up works well for this one, where

viewers can see what you're doing as well as how well you're managing to perform in the game.

Top Tips

Double check the camera is recording – this is one gaming video you won't want to have to repeat.

Watch

Impossible Let's Play: TREADMILL CHALLENGE – Markiplier

☐ **Video completed**

Date ___/____/____

NOTES:...
....
....

GAMING INSPIRATION

46. GAMING SET-UP TOUR

No matter what your set-up, viewers are always interested to see the specific gaming products you use and the place where all the action happens.

Prepare
Make sure your gaming area is tidy and think about any items you'd specifically like to talk about and what you will say about them. This kind of video is especially useful to anyone who's thinking of starting up their own gaming channel, so think of any useful tips you can include too.

Film
Give your viewers a 'behind the scenes' tour of your gaming area and set-up. Go into detail about your gaming computer, any consoles you use, your capture card, microphone set-up, headphones and editing software.

Top Tips
You could think of this as a kind of product review – tell viewers why you use each of your gaming items, what they do and the things you like and dislike about them.

Watch
My Setup Tour!
– jacksepticeye

☐ **Video completed**
Date ____/____/____

NOTES:..
....
....

47. GAMING NEWS

Make this a weekly update on your channel to become your subscribers' go-to source for all the latest video game news and knowledge.

Prepare
You'll have to do some research for this video before you start to film. Keep up-to-date with current trends, game release dates, new trailers, the latest technology and even what's going on in the YouTube gaming community itself.

Film
Present your information to camera in an informative and professional way, kind of like a television news reporter would do. Do, however, feel free to inject your own opinions and sense of humour to make the video your own and show off your personality to any new viewers.

Top Tips
You could collect info from gaming websites such as PC Gamer and Gamespot, gaming-specific magazines, game developers, technology sites, top YouTube gaming channels and Twitter accounts.

Watch
Ubisoft #1 in 2017! -
The Know Game
News – The Know

☐ **Video completed**
Date ____/____/____

NOTES:..
....
....

GAMING INSPIRATION

48. GAME GLITCHES

From rogue body parts to flying animals, invisible walls and demon babies, glitch-ridden games make for some of the funniest viewing on YouTube.

Prepare
Pick a game that doesn't work. This is a sure fire way to make sure you end up with plenty of ridiculous moments. Games such as Goat Simulator and Sonic '06 are full of glitchy gold. In fact, since this type of video is so big, some games developers have even started to make games that are full of silly glitches on purpose.

Film
Record your gameplay every time you play, whether it's for fun or filming. After logging a few hours you're bound to end up with enough quality clips to make up a short montage video.

Top Tips
Edit and organise your footage after each gaming session while it's still fresh in your mind. This will make it much easier to compile all your best glitch clips when you get round to actually making the video.

Watch
Top 10 Funniest Glitches in Video Games! – PBG – PeanutButterGamer

☐ **Video completed**
Date ___/___/___

NOTES:..
....
....

49. HOW-TO/TUTORIAL

If you're a bit of a pro at one particular game, why not upload a how-to video offering others a hand with the tricky parts.

Prepare
Think of an idea that would make for a good tutorial. It could be something you struggled with in a game and managed to complete, or simply a skill that you're really good at and want to show off.

Film
How-to gaming videos are usually more specific than a walkthrough, so keep filming focused on just one part of the game, whether that's teaching viewers how to unlock an obscure achievement, explaining a confusing part or showing off advanced techniques for skilled players.

Top Tips
Once you've built up your channel, regularly check the comments as viewers may ask you for help with a game. You can then turn the question and your solution to it into a whole new video.

Watch
FIFA 16 Tutorial - Advanced Skill Moves - Spin Flick, Elastico, Elastico Chop – EA SPORTS FIFA

☐ **Video completed**
Date ___/___/___

NOTES:..
....
....

GAMING INSPIRATION

50. VIDEO GAME ANALYSIS

This is your chance to get your geek on and explore games on a whole other level. From in-depth discussions about themes to fan theories and all kinds of interesting trivia, you get to analyse your fave games from the inside out.

Prepare
These videos are basically like online essays, so that's what you'll need to do: prepare a structured essay to act as your script. This might sound super boring but many people are interested to hear unique perspectives on popular video games.

Film
Since this is a scripted video you'll need to record your voiceover. Insert it over footage of whichever game you choose to talk about – either clips that back up your argument or just in-game footage.

Top Tips
Although the content in these videos is more educational, it still needs to be entertaining. Try to keep your commentary lively, enthusiastic and engaging, and avoid speaking in a monotone.

Watch
Mari Geek Remix Video Game Theories (Playlist) – Geek Remix

☐ **Video completed**

Date ____/____/____

NOTES:...
....
....

51. MACHINIMA

If you love movies just as much as you love games, this is the perfect video for you. For Machinima, or "machine cinema", creators use existing game graphics to create their own awesome works of art.

Prepare
Pick a game and start to write out a script based around the characters and settings available. Popular games to use for Machinima include Halo, The Sims, WoW and Grand Theft Auto – basically any game where you can control the movements of different characters.

Film
To make your Machinima, you'll capture and edit in-game footage to create your own mini movie. Enlist friends to play different character roles and finish recording the dialogue first. You can then act

out the parts in-game, controlling the characters like your own digital puppets.

Top Tips
Watch lots of other Machinimas first to see how it's done and get inspiration for your own.

Watch
Why Are We Here? – Episode 1 – Red vs. Blue Season 1 – Red vs. Blue

☐ **Video completed**

Date ____/____/____

NOTES:...
....
....

GAMING INSPIRATION

52. HAPPY WHEELS

The delightfully destructive game Happy Wheels hit the Internet in 2010 and to say it's done wheelie well on YouTube would be an understatement. We say make your own video and jump on that bandwagon... or bicycle... or wheelchair...

Prepare
The beauty of this browser game is that it's simple to play and 100% free, so you'll hardly need to do any prep at all. There's now even an official app version too.

Film
Set up your screen recording and get rolling. Happy Wheels Let's Play videos with live reactions have done very well for the likes of PewDiePie, jacksepticeye, TobyGames and Markiplier, but put your own spin on it too.

Top Tips
Have a laugh. If you're not having fun while you're playing the game then nobody else is going to have fun watching you play it.

Watch
Happy Wheels - Part 100 (GRAND FINALE) – jacksepticeye

☐ **Video completed**

Date ___/___/___

NOTES:..
....
....

53. MAKE A GAMING MUSIC VIDEO

One of the most creative types of gaming videos. Gaming-themed music videos are always fun and can even end up going viral.

Prepare
Decide which game to make a music video for. You can either create your own original song or make a musical parody using a well-known song. You'll then need to write some lyrics – the funnier the better.

Film
You could make an animated Minecraft parody video based on a popular song, write your own rap or make like Markiplier and film your own video-game themed musical.

Top Tips
Think about popular games and current trends when deciding which game to base your song around. CaptainSparklez' song parodies about Minecraft are some of the most viewed gaming videos on YouTube.

Watch
"Revenge" - A Minecraft Original Music Video – CaptainSparklez

☐ **Video completed**

Date ___/___/___

NOTES:..
....
....

GAMING INSPIRATION

54. SCARY GAMES

What better time to freak yourself out playing Five Nights at Freddy's than on the spookiest night of the year? Horror games make for some truly funny reactions and as a result propelled gamers like PewDiePie to stardom.

Prepare
Pick a survival horror game to play. Amnesia, Slender and Five Nights at Freddy's have all proved to be prime material for jump scares, screaming and sheer terror.

Film
Get your reaction cam ready, set up the stream and prepare to scream.

Top Tips
As well as playing the big name games, look out for newer, less played horror releases too. This way, viewers who want to see just how terrifying they are will be more likely to stumble across your channel.

Complete this video in time for Halloween

Watch
WARNING: YOU WILL DIE | Five Nights at Freddy's 3 - Part 1 – Markiplier

☐ **Video completed**
Date ____/____/____

NOTES:...
....
....

55. HOUSE BUILDS

Tap into your inner interior designer and impress new viewers with a vlog showing off your virtual house builds.

Prepare
Choose an open world game that allows you to build something spectacular. From decorating your dream home in The Sims to making an entire castle in Minecraft, you'll find endless opportunities to get creative.

Film
Think of your video like a virtual room tour. Show viewers your build and talk through the different rooms, the items you used, plans for future improvements and offer any tips and tricks. You could also do a live video where you customise your house on camera.

Top Tips
Some gamers have made the record books for their impressive Minecraft builds, creating hugely detailed simulations of movie worlds and real life buildings. This takes a LOT of time to achieve but is almost guaranteed to get views.

Watch
"MY TREE HOUSE" Minecraft Enchanted Oasis Ep 2 – iHasCupquake

☐ **Video completed**
Date ____/____/____

NOTES:...
....
....

GAMING INSPIRATION

56. COMPUTER GAMES IRL

Comedy videos about gaming are practically as popular as straight gaming videos themselves. A good way to get people laughing is by bringing your favourite computer games and characters to life.

Prepare
Imagine what your favourite games would look like in real life and the kinds of ridiculous situations the characters would get themselves into. Turn your ideas into a funny script for a comedy sketch and get creative with homemade cosplay costumes.

Film
Cast your friends in different video game character roles, get dressed up and have a blast playing director for the day.

Top Tips
Pick well-known characters that people know and love and include plenty of in-jokes poking fun at the games.

Watch
If Video Games Were Real – Smosh

☐ **Video completed**
Date ____/____/____

NOTES:..
....
....

57. MULTIPLAYER

Collaborating with other gamers will not only help your channel to grow but also keep content fresh and interesting. After all, more players = more fun.

Prepare
Build relationships with other gaming creators you admire before thinking about creative ways you could collaborate with each other in a video. Multiplayer videos usually make for an entertaining watch thanks to fun commentaries, catchphrases and lots of friendly banter.

Film
You don't need to be in the same location as the other player, but you do need to make sure you are both recording your audio, which you can easily do using free software such as Audacity. The trick is to then sync up the audio tracks with your game footage during editing. Communicate clearly and try not to talk over each other too much.

Top Tips
Sometimes the YouTube collaboration works out so well that the creators decide to form a new channel together. Take a look at GameGrumps, for example.

Watch
Monopoly - Game Grumps VS – GameGrumps

☐ **Video completed**
Date ____/____/____

NOTES:..
....
....

GAMING INSPIRATION

58. PLAY AN UNKNOWN GAME

Don't film all the same big name games that everybody else is playing – choose something under the radar. You never know, you could be the trendsetter who discovers the next Goat Simulator...

Prepare
Whether it's a new indie release, a retro game or something that's so terrible it's good, think outside the box when it comes to picking your next game. Plus, games that don't already have lots of Let's Plays are easier to make your own content about.

Film
Make whichever video you think will showcase the game best, whether that's a walkthrough, a collab with friends or a funny first reaction.

Top Tips
Though it's tempting to only review and play popular games to get more views, some small indie games can suddenly take off on YouTube and become super influential. If you already have videos up you'll be ahead of the crowd.

Watch
I am Bread - First Look – Bossa Studios

☐ **Video completed**
Date ___/___/___

NOTES:...
....
....

59. GAMING EXPO VLOG

Major gaming conventions and eSports tournaments take place throughout the year. If you're lucky enough to be able to get to one, don't miss the opportunity to make an exciting vlog about it.

Prepare
Look online to see if there are any cool conventions, talks or gaming events going on near you. Some of the biggest events in the gaming calendar include the E3 Expo, EGX and GamesCon.

Film
Take your video camera with you and remember to vlog throughout the day, almost as if you were making a day in the life video. Give unique coverage of unmissable talks, sneak peeks, meet and greets with gamers and generally share the excitement with your viewers.

Top Tips
If you're not able to attend an event, never fear! YouTube Gaming offers live stream coverage from big gaming events like E3. Keep an eye on it for any big announcements and you could make your very own news vlog covering the best bits.

Watch
E3 Youtuber Meetup and Gaming Convention! (Vlog w/ Godson) – Godson – Clash Gaming

☐ **Video completed**
Date ___/___/___

NOTES:...
....

GAMING INSPIRATION

60. SPORTS TOURNAMENT

Bring out your competitive side by inviting your pals round for the ultimate sporting competition – minus any real exercise, of course.

Prepare

Whether it's a goal-scoring contest in Fifa, a silly sports simulator or battling it out at the Wii Sports Resort, pick a competitive sports game that'll leave you and your mates laughing.

Film

Set up a camera to film the room you're using, check that the angle is wide enough to fit everyone in shot. You'll also need to capture the on-screen footage in order to edit both sets of footage together later. Now, let the games begin.

Top Tips

If you're an editing whizz, place a window on screen for each player including their name and picture, and keep a running tally of the scores here throughout the video.

Watch

Dan Phil Felix and Marzia play REALISTIC SUMMER SPORTS SIMULATOR! – DanAndPhilGAMES

☐ **Video completed**

Date ___/___/___

NOTES:...
....
....

61. TOP 10 GAMES

Complete this video at the end of the year

Top 10 lists are currently a very popular video format on YouTube. They're easy to put together and are almost guaranteed to bring in new viewers who are looking for a list of great new games to play.

Prepare

Choose a topic for your list. It could be your top video games of all time or a top 10 of video game characters, bosses, graphics – the list goes on.

Film

Talk through your list, starting at number 10 and counting down towards 1, briefly explaining the reasons why each item deserves its position in the list. A good way to start a discussion with your subscribers is by asking them to comment at the end with what would have made their top 10 lists.

Top Tips

This is the perfect video idea to upload on New Year's Eve, letting viewers know what has made it on to your 'Top 10 Games of the Year' list.

Watch

Top 10 Video Games of All Time – WatchMojo.com

☐ **Video completed**

Date ___/___/___

NOTES:...
....
....

GAMING INSPIRATION

62. EASTER EGGS

The ideal upload for Easter time, this is a video uncovering all the Easter eggs and secrets hidden in your favourite games.

Prepare
Developers often stuff their games full of 'Easter eggs' for players to find, from inside jokes to sneaky messages, secret features and hidden endings. If you haven't discovered enough of your own Easter eggs in a game, there's enough information online to use to create your own easy-to-watch list.

Film
Document your Easter egg knowledge through game play footage and record a voiceover to go with it, sharing instructions on how to find them as well as including any interesting facts or hacks.

Top Tips
You could also turn this into an awesome 'Top 10' video, listing ten different Easter eggs hidden in ten different games.

Complete this video during the Easter break

Watch
Mario Part 1 - Easter Egg Hunting – DidYouKnowGaming?

☐ **Video completed**
Date ____/____/____

NOTES:...
....
....

63. LIVE STREAM

Streaming is a great way to grow your channel. Since the introduction of its own dedicated gaming platform, YouTube Gaming, it's never been easier to live stream content to your loyal subscribers.

Prepare
Have an idea what you're going to do and a few talking points before starting the live stream. There's no editing out your bad bits here. Generally, live streams are the place to play competitive games in real time while also interacting with your viewers.

Film
Once you are ready, go to youtube.com/gaming on your web browser. Sign into your YouTube account and click GO LIVE at the top of the homepage. Once you're on the Stream Now page, click to Get Started and you're ready to roll.

Top Tips
Live streams might seem scary but they are a big thing in the gaming world. Wait until you've built up a few subscribers and have enough videos under your belt to be comfortable talking on demand.

Watch

Black Ops 3: Zombies: 'REVELATIONS' First Live Attempt! – TheSyndicateProject

☐ **Video completed**
Date ____/____/____

NOTES:...
....
....

GAMING IDEAS

Think up 10 of your own ideas for gaming videos to film. Maybe you've discovered a new gaming app you think other people would love, or you fancy challenging your mates to a time trial or you just want to show off your in-game inventories.

64

65

66

67

68

69

70

71

72

73

NOTES:

GAMING NOTES

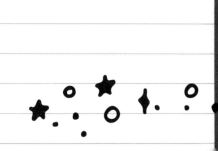

FASHION & BEAUTY

From makeup tutorials to massive hauls, seasonal lookbooks to how-to styling tips, people all over the world are turning to YouTube for all their fashion and beauty needs. Whether you're a budding beauty guru or a fashionista in the making, there are plenty of video ideas and tutorials that are guaranteed to help your subscribers up their style.

CHANNEL INSPIRATION:

Tanya Burr: From easy-to-follow celeb makeup looks to current beauty trends, huge fashion hauls, hairstyles and even baking, Tanya Burr has a video for everything.

Samantha Maria: As you might expect from a fashion grad turned designer, Samantha Maria's channel is packed full of style. Check her out for slickly edited lookbooks, chatty hauls, monthly favourites and all kinds of advice.

NikkieTutorials: With her expert makeup tips and flawless tutorials full of colour, glamour and all things glitter, NikkieTutorials is the girl to turn to if you need a master class in makeup.

FASHION & BEAUTY INSPIRATION

74. THE HAUL

The haul is probably the most popular fashion and beauty video of all. If you love to shop till you drop, show viewers your shiny new purchases to provide a never-ending supply of shopping inspiration.

Prepare
Save up your purchases from a recent shopping splurge and think about the kind of haul video you can make. It could be a shop-specific haul (if all your items are from the same place), one that's relevant to the time of year, or just one big blowout.

Film
Show off your items one by one. Explain why you picked each one, where you got it from, how much it was and the ways you're planning to wear or use it.

Top Tips
For maximum viewers, upload your haul videos during popular times of the year and title it accordingly. Show off your summer clothes haul at the start of the holidays and do a back to school haul at the end.

Watch
HUGE Beauty & Fashion Haul! | Tanya Burr – Tanya Burr

☐ **Video completed**
Date ___/___/___

NOTES:...
....
....

75. WHAT'S IN MY BAG?

Give viewers an insight into your life by letting them see the contents of your handbag, or your backpack, or bumbag... whatever you carry around with you. You get the idea.

Prepare
Make sure your bag is ready before filming. It should be the everyday bag you're currently using, filled with all the usual items you like to have with you when you're out and about.

Film
Go through your bag on camera, pulling out items one-by-one. From essential cosmetics to electronics, pretty purses and personal items, talk about each item and why it's in your bag.

Top Tips
If you're a budding beauty guru, you could make another version of this video and show subscribers what's in your makeup bag, too.

Watch
What's In My Purse? Carli Bybel – Carli Bybel

☐ **Video completed**
Date ___/___/___

NOTES:...
....
....

FASHION & BEAUTY INSPIRATION

76. BEAUTY TUTORIAL

Makeup tutorials are among the most viewed videos on YouTube. Show off your makeup skills and teach viewers how to pull off a totally polished look from start to finish.

Prepare
Plan out the look you want to create before filming your tutorial. Lay out all the beauty products and tools you'll need to create your look and make sure they're in easy reach of the camera.

Film
Starting with a makeup free face, go through the look step-by-step (usually using a voiceover), showing the products you're using and explaining how you're using them. Be encouraging – the finished look should seem achievable enough for your viewers to recreate at home.

Top Tips
It's a good idea to show the finished makeup look within the first 10 seconds of your video to get viewers interested to watch the rest.

Watch
Easy Glam HOLIDAY Makeup Tutorial! | Lauren Curtis – Lauren Curtis

☐ **Video completed**
Date ___/___/____

NOTES:..
....
....

77. OUTFIT OF THE DAY

Satisfy any viewers looking for some fashion inspiration by showing off your perfectly put together outfit of the day.

Prepare
Whether you're all dressed up for a special occasion or just think your ensemble is particularly on-point one day, film this video when you're wearing an outfit worth sharing. Seeing other people put together an outfit in a new and unique way can give viewers the confidence to shake up their own style.

Film
Show off your outfit from every angle, including close-up details and full-length shots. A great OOTD shows clothes at their best and leaves viewers excited to put together their own looks, so make sure you include information to recreate the look.

Top Tips
If you film your outfit of the day every day for a week you can then compile the footage into an 'outfit of the week' or 'what I wore in a week' video, like an online fashion diary.

Watch
WHAT I WORE THIS WEEK | Samantha Maria – Samantha Maria

☐ **Video completed**
Date ___/___/____

NOTES:..
....
....

FASHION & BEAUTY INSPIRATION

78. THE LOOKBOOK

Viewers love to watch lookbooks to keep up with the latest trends and see what's in the shops. Make your own lookbook by modelling a few outfits you've lovingly put together.

Prepare
Plan out the outfits you'll show based around an overall theme. For example, lookbooks usually show the upcoming trends for each season or month. Whatever the trend or season, make sure to keep true to your style, as that's what viewers want to see.

Film
Ask a friend to film you, as you show off each of your outfits in different poses and even different locations. It's basically like a live action photoshoot. Include close-ups of details and information about where the items are from and how much they cost.

Top Tips
Watch a few other fashion vloggers' videos for inspiration. Lookbooks are usually highly stylised, with a soundtrack but no voiceover,. though of course you can come up with your own way to film yours.

Watch
5 Fall Trends Lookbook – clothesencounters

☐ **Video completed**
Date ____/____/____

NOTES:...
....
....

79. THREE MINUTE MAKEUP CHALLENGE

An oldie but always a goody, the aim of this challenge is to complete an entire face of makeup, as well as you can, in three minutes or under.

Prepare
Lay out all the makeup products you'll need before filming and make sure they're within easy reach of the camera. Have your products open ready to use and take tops off of bottles to save time. It may sound easy enough, but it's amazing how quickly three minutes flies.

Film
Make sure your camera's rolling, set your timer to three minutes, grab a makeup brush and the challenge is on. Add a countdown clock to the screen

so viewers can see how much time you have too.

Top Tips
Don't worry if your makeup is not perfect at the end. One of the best things about this challenge is to see the look of panic on people's faces as they realise they're running out of time.

Watch
3 MINUTE MAKEUP CHALLENGE! – bubzbeauty

☐ **Video completed**
Date ____/____/____

NOTES:...
....
....

FASHION & BEAUTY INSPIRATION

80. MY DAILY MAKEUP ROUTINE

Super glam looks are all well and good, but viewers are often interested to get a behind-the-scenes glimpse at how their fave vloggers achieve their everyday look.

Prepare
Choose the makeup you reach for to get ready on a daily basis, whether it's your go-to look for lazy days or going to school.

Film
Film yourself as you carry out your usual makeup routine, sharing the essential products you use each day and how you use them. Also share any tricks you've picked up that make your beauty routine easier and save you time in the morning.

Top Tips
It's very important to have good lighting in these videos in order to fully show off the final results. Natural lighting is best, so try to sit near a window and film your videos early in the day. A ring light is also a good investment for beauty vloggers.

Watch
My Everyday Makeup Routine! 2017 – Claudia Sulewski

☐ **Video completed**

Date ___/___/___

NOTES:...
....
....

81. FIRST IMPRESSIONS

First impressions videos help viewers by taking the guesswork out of buying beauty products. Film your own video testing out new makeup products for the very first time and tell your viewers what you think.

Prepare
Wait until you have a few new beauty products you want to try so you can test them out all at once in front of the camera. This way, viewers get to see your genuine reactions, whether they're great or not so good.

Film
Make a chatty, informal video, simply talking through each of the new products as you use them to create a makeup look in front of the camera. Share your initial impressions, giving viewers the lowdown on the ones you loved and the ones you didn't.

Top Tips
It's a good idea to zoom the camera in to your face as you apply makeup to different areas. This will allow viewers to get a better idea of what the products look like on.

Watch
FULL FACE OF FIRST IMPRESSIONS MAKEUP TUTORIAL | Jaclyn Hill – Jaclyn Hill

☐ **Video completed**

Date ___/___/___

NOTES:...
....
....

FASHION & BEAUTY INSPIRATION

82. WARDROBE TOUR & ORGANISATION

Perfect for any super tidy YouTuber, this video gives you the chance to take viewers on a tour of your closet and share your top organisation tips.

Prepare
Make sure your wardrobe is tidy and organised before filming. Or, if it needs a bit of work, clear it out on camera and make that the focus of your video instead.

Film
Walk viewers through your wardrobe space, giving a peek behind doors and into drawers, pointing out any essential items. Talk about how you keep it in order and share any tips and tricks that could help others organise their own closets too.

Top Tips
Videos where vloggers show off their makeup collection storage solutions are also very requested on YouTube.

Watch
Closet Organization Tips & Tour! – Nastazsa

☐ **Video completed**

Date ____/____/____

NOTES:...
....
....

---

83. GET READY WITH ME

A GRWM is a combination of a routine video and a makeup tutorial. Film this video when you're getting glammed up for a special occasion to show viewers how you get ready from head to toe.

Prepare
Put some thought into the look before filming. Whether you're getting ready for a birthday do, prom night or to go back to school, you'll need to show viewers your full getting ready process, including hair, makeup and final outfit.

Film
Film yourself getting ready in real time, showing your routine step-by-step from start to finish. Make sure you include all the products you use and the rest is up to you. Some GRWM's have a voiceover, some are chatty and some simply have a soundtrack.

Top Tips
Most vloggers speed up certain parts of the video (like blending foundation and filling in brows) to keep the video from getting too long.

Watch
Get Ready with Me: Night with Friends! – Amanda Steele

☐ **Video completed**

Date ____/____/____

NOTES:...
....
....

FASHION & BEAUTY INSPIRATION

84. NAIL ART TUTORIAL

If you're pretty nifty at painting your nails, why not turn your talents into a video? Upload a nail tutorial teaching viewers how they too can apply polish like a pro.

Prepare
Come up with a fun and creative nail art design that any viewer will be able to recreate at home, whether they're a nail novice or not. Next, prep your nails and get your tools and polishes ready.

Film
Set up your camera to film your hands from above as you paint your nails and apply your designs. Add a voiceover to your video afterwards, sharing your step-by-step techniques to achieve the perfect polish.

Top Tips
You'll need some good editing to keep this tutorial to the point – nobody wants to sit and watch nail paint dry! A good rule of thumb is to keep beauty tutorials at around 6-8 minutes or shorter.

Watch
10 Easy Nail Art Designs for Beginners: The Ultimate Guide #4! – cutepolish

☐ **Video completed**

Date ___/___/___

NOTES:...
....
....

---

85. PRODUCT REVIEWS

Ever bought a product that wasn't worth your hard-earned bucks? Help others avoid beauty mistakes and pick up great products by uploading your own honest and helpful product reviews.

Prepare
Depending on whether you loved or hated a product, you might include it in a favourites round up or a 'Products I Regret Buying' video. Or, create a review video focusing on just one product.

Film
Show the products to the camera, sharing your genuine opinions about each one. If you're reviewing a makeup item make sure you include swatches or, even better, show what the product looks like on. As always, include links to all the products mentioned.

Top Tips
The most trusted beauty vloggers are those who are consistently honest in their reviews and provide useful advice about products, considering the types of people who would and would not like them. If your video has been sponsored by a brand, you must let your viewers know.

Watch
DISAPPOINTINPRODUCTS – Caroline Hirons

☐ **Video completed**

Date ___/___/___

NOTES:...
....
....

FASHION & BEAUTY INSPIRATION

86. VALENTINE'S DAY LOOK

Complete this video for February 14th

Make a how-to video and give your viewers a helping hand when it comes to wowing their dates on Valentine's Day.

Prepare
Whether it's an amazing outfit idea, hairstyle inspiration, knockout nails or a pretty makeup look, pick a video idea that'll help your viewers look their best on their special date.

Film
Film an instructional tutorial to help viewers achieve your Valentine's inspired look, taking them through the products they'll need and how to do it. Make sure you upload your video at least a week before February 14th!

Top Tips
Valentine's content is big news on YT. Make sure your video can be found by titling and tagging it properly. Be sure to include the type of content you're doing, the date and other important info in your tags.

Watch
Valentine's Day Makeup Chatty GRWM | Jessica Clements – Jessica Clements

☐ **Video completed**

Date ___/___/___

NOTES:..
....
....

87. THE OUTFIT CHALLENGE

Team up with a friend or family member and test how well you know each other's style by taking on the outfit challenge.

Prepare
Set yourselves a budget to go shopping with and each buy an entire outfit for the other person. The winner of the challenge is the one who picked out the clothes that best fit the other person's fashion sense.

Film
Sit together in front of the camera and take it in turns to reveal your chosen clothing items one at a time. Afterwards, try on each of your outfits, filming them in the same way as you would for an outfit of the day.

Top Tips
Don't forget to interact with your viewers by asking them to leave a comment and let you know which outfit they thought was best at the end of the video.

Watch
£50 OUTFIT CHALLENGE WITH ROXXSAURUS – Inthefrow

☐ **Video completed**

Date ___/___/___

NOTES:..
....
....

FASHION & BEAUTY INSPIRATION

88. QUICK & EASY HAIRSTYLES

Provide your viewers with enough quick and easy hairdo tutorials to become the YouTuber they turn to on every bad hair day.

Prepare
Pick a few of your favourite hairstyles and practice them to perfection. From no heat hairstyles to messy buns, beach waves and every braid imaginable, there are plenty of styles to choose.

Film
Teach viewers how to recreate your hairstyles at home, slowly taking them through the style step-by-step. Hairstyles can sometimes seem tricky to do so offer plenty of encouragement and make your instructions as clear as possible.

Top Tips
Set your camera up on a tripod and make sure you turn your head so viewers can see what you're doing from every angle as you carry out the hairstyle. Or, ask a friend to be a hair model for you.

Watch
QUICK AND EASY HAIRSTYLES – Jordan Lipscombe

☐ **Video completed**

Date ___/____/____

NOTES:...
....
....

89. EMPTY PRODUCTS

Easy to make and enjoyable to watch, empty product videos put trash to good use and show vloggers giving their tried, tested and true reviews of all the items they've used up.

Prepare
Over the course of a month (or longer) collect all of the empty beauty products you'd usually bin – you'll need these to make your video. Viewers love to see empties reviews because, unlike First Impressions videos, the items have been tried and tested until the end.

Film
Go through your empty bottles and containers and give a quick review of each product, telling viewers whether it was good or not and whether you're going to repurchase it.

Top Tips
Getting passionate about the products you love will really help show off your personality. Since this video is all about the items you've liked well enough to finish, there should be a few favourites for you to rave about.

Watch
EMPTIES | Stuff I've Used Up – Samantha Maria

☐ **Video completed**

Date ___/____/____

NOTES:...
....
....

FASHION & BEAUTY INSPIRATION

90. MAKEUP TIPS & TECHNIQUES

If you're a dab hand at doing your makeup, share your secrets to help others looking to step up their makeup skills.

Prepare
These videos are different to get ready tutorials in that they usually focus on teaching viewers one specific trick to get their makeup looks picture perfect. Pick something you're great at to make a tutorial about, whether that's applying the perfect winged eyeliner or putting on falsies in a flash.

Film
Break down the makeup technique into easy-to-manage steps, explaining which products, tools and techniques you use to achieve the look.

Top Tips
Keep on top of the hottest makeup trends and try to make tutorials on them. When viewers want to find out how to do the latest dewy skin look or brow trend, they'll find your top tips first.

Watch
HOW TO CONTOUR AND HIGHLIGHT LIKE KIM KARDASHIAN – Wayne Goss

☐ **Video completed**

Date ____/____/____

NOTES:..
....
....

91. STEAL CELEB STYLE

Some of the most-watched fashion and beauty videos are 'get the look' tutorials based on popular celebrities. Make your own video teaching viewers how to steal the style of the stars.

Prepare
Whether it's Gigi Hadid, Selena Gomez or Kendall and Kylie, pick a celeb whose style you love and use them as your inspiration to create a similar look. Of course, celeb wardrobes are usually out of the average person's price range, so this video is all about how you can recreate their style on a budget.

Film
Use your celebspiration to film a step-by-step tutorial teaching viewers how to recreate red carpet-worthy hair, outfit and makeup looks for less.

Top Tips
Along the same lines, tutorial videos inspired by popular characters from films and TV shows also do well on YouTube. You could recreate the look of your favourite Pretty Little Liar or Disney character, too.

Watch
GET THE LOOK: ARIANA GRANDE | 2017 Outfits for Less – Tess Christine

☐ **Video completed**

Date ____/____/____

NOTES:..
....
....

FASHION & BEAUTY INSPIRATION

92. TRY-ON CLOTHES HAUL

The latest trend for clothing hauls is the Try-On Haul. Viewers often like to see what clothes look like on someone else before they buy, so try this video on your channel next time you have a haul.

Prepare
Save up your recently purchased clothing items, just as you would do for a regular haul video. Remember to keep note of where you bought each item from and how much it cost.

Film
Discuss each item in front of the camera before trying the clothes on and include a full-length shot showing what they look like. Move around so viewers can see how the clothes fit and also mention which size you got.

Top Tips
It's also a good idea to style up the items during the try on, demonstrating how each of the clothing items can be worn with other things in your wardrobe.

Watch
HUGE SUMMER TRY ON HAUL | Bethany Mota – Bethany Mota

☐ **Video completed**

Date ____/____/____

NOTES:..
....
....

93. HALLOWEEN MAKEUP

If you have mad skills with a makeup brush, Halloween is the perfect time to get creative with spooky beauty looks and horrifying special effects.

Prepare
These are not your basic beauty looks, so be prepared to practise before filming. Come up with an out-of-the-ordinary makeup look that would be perfect for a Halloween party, whether that's a creepy character transformation, realistic special effects or blood and gore galore.

Film
Talk viewers through your transformation process as you create the look from start to finish. Since these tutorials are usually more complex than a normal beauty look, you'll need to make sure your instructions are clear.

Top Tips
These videos can take some time to film (and a very steady hand) but since Halloween makeup looks are the most searched for beauty tutorials of the year, the results will be worth it.

Complete this video in the run-up to Halloween

Watch
Speak No Evil - Zombie Mouth Special FX Makeup Tutorial – Glam&Gore

☐ **Video completed**

Date ____/____/____

NOTES:..
....
....

FASHION & BEAUTY INSPIRATION

94. HAULTERNATIVE

Complete this video during Fashion Revolution Week

Fashion Revolution Week (April) aims to challenge conditions in the fashion industry and promote ethical alternatives to fast, disposable fashion. Raise awareness by making your own #haulternative video.

Prepare
#Haulternatives prove that you don't need to buy new clothes to enjoy a good old haul. Check out the different kinds of haulternatives you can do to refresh your wardrobe without buying anything brand new, and pick one that inspires you.

Film
Get your camera out and film your thrifty haul. From a clothes swap with friends to showing off your favourite second-hand shopping finds and fashion fix DIYs, there are plenty of fun ideas to try.

Top Tips
If you care about where your clothing comes from, share information with your viewers about Fashion Revolution and how they too can get involved with the cause. Share your video on social media and get people talking.

Watch
HAULTERNATIVE | Marzia's Style – Marzia

☐ **Video completed**

Date ____/____/____

NOTES:...
....
....

95. BUDGET BEAUTY

We all love a beauty bargain, so why not share your best drugstore beauty finds with the world?

Prepare
Whether it's amazing mascaras, lippies, nail polishes or powders, dig out the drugstore beauty products that have made it to holy grail status in your makeup bag. You could categorise the video by beauty product, brand, or just do one big overview.

Film
Talk through your beauty bargains one by one and tell viewers why you love them and what you use them for. You could even create a full makeup look using only high-street products to show how well they work.

Top Tips
Other variations of this video include 'High Street vs. High End' videos where vloggers compare luxury beauty items with budget dupes, and undertake the $20 Makeup Challenge.

Watch
13 Drugstore Products I LOVE! – AndreasChoice

☐ **Video completed**

Date ____/____/____

NOTES:...
....
....

FASHION & BEAUTY INSPIRATION

96. YOUTUBE MADE ME BUY IT

Since most of us spend a lot of time on YouTube, we're bound to pick up a few things that come recommended by our fave creators. Kind of like a product review in reverse, make a video shouting out all the things YouTube made you buy.

Prepare
Think of all the beauty products and clothing items you've bought because you saw them recommended or used on YouTube and gather them up to use in your video.

Film
Show off each product you've bought and talk about whether or not it lived up to the hype. This video is also a great way to give a shout-out to the fashion and beauty gurus you love to watch, so don't forget to mention who made you buy it.

Top Tips
You can also mention products you haven't bought yet but are on your wish list thanks to YouTube.

Watch
Youtube Made Me Buy It! Tag | Beauty Products I Bought BECAUSE OF YT HYPE! – KathleenLights

☐ **Video completed**

Date ____/____/____

NOTES:...
....

97. THE POWER OF MAKEUP

The Power of Makeup challenge aims to not only show what a difference makeup can make, but also to take a stand against the makeup shamers. Embrace both sides of yourself – made-up and makeup free – by uploading your own.

Prepare
The challenge was first posted by NikkieTutorials and quickly caught on – check out her video for inspiration before making your own.

Film
You'll need to film yourself as you apply a glam makeup look to only one half of your face, leaving the other half totally bare. Treat it like a makeup tutorial and talk through what you're doing as you go.

Top Tips
This is one makeup tutorial where you shouldn't show the finished look at the beginning of the video – leave the final transformation reveal till the end to keep viewers watching!

Watch
The Power of MAKEUP! – NikkieTutorials

☐ **Video completed**

Date ____/____/____

NOTES:...
....
....

FASHION & BEAUTY INSPIRATION

98. BOYFRIEND DOES MY VOICEOVER

This latest tag trend is all the rage. Asking your boyfriend or male friend to narrate your video will make for one hilarious makeup tutorial with a twist.

Prepare

Beg or bribe your boyfriend to take part in your video – all he has to do is record a voiceover to a makeup tutorial describing what he thinks you're doing.

Film

Film yourself creating a makeup look. Once you've edited it, get your boyfriend to watch it and record the voiceover.

Watch
♥ BOYFRIEND DOES MY VOICE OVER! ft. DOGMAN ♥ – grav3yardgirl

☐ **Video completed**

Date ___/___/___

99. MOTHER'S DAY MAKEOVER

Treat your mother like the queen she is with a Mother's Day makeover. It's the perfect excuse to make a video and make your mum happy too.

Prepare

Decide how you'll pamper your mother. It could be a new makeup look or hairstyle, a full makeover or vlogging a shopping trip for a new outfit.

Film

Film your video as you would a tutorial or get ready with me, just with the added extra of having your mum as your model.

Watch
Power of Makeup (Mother-in-law Makeover) – dope2111

☐ **Video completed**

Date ___/___/___

100. ERA INSPIRED LOOKS

Take your viewers on a trip down history lane with looks inspired by different eras of time, from the Roaring Twenties to the Swinging Sixties.

Prepare

Whether you're creating a makeup tutorial or an era-inspired lookbook, you'll need to do some research into the time period you've chosen to see what looks were on trend.

Film

Film a video incorporating aspects of the era into the look you recreate, and tell viewers how they can get the look too.

Watch
70's Look | Makeup, Hair & Outfit | MsRosieBea – MsRosieBea

☐ **Video completed**

Date ___/___/___

FASHION & BEAUTY IDEAS

Fill in another 10 ideas for even more fashion and beauty content to film. You could put together your own seasonal lookbook, do a prom makeup tutorial, or even come up with a brand new beauty tag.

101 ....
....
....
....

102 ....
....
....
....

103 ....
....
....
....

104 ....
....
....
....

105 ....
....
....
....

106

107

108

109

110

NOTES:

FASHION & BEAUTY NOTES

CHALLENGES

From hilarious physical feats to the downright dangerous, the trend for YouTube challenge videos is going nowhere. Challenge creators regularly team up to test their limits to the max; taking on all manner of outrageous and hilarious dares just to keep their viewers entertained. So, if you think you've got what it takes, grab a camera, grab your pals, and get competing.

CHANNEL INSPIRATION:

Oli White: British YouTuber Oli White loves nothing more than to entertain subscribers with his silly but hilarious challenge videos, featuring collabs with his fellow vlogging friends, family and celebs alike.

Wassabi Productions: Whether it's taking ice baths or eating truly disgusting foods, Alex Wassabi will take on any and every entertaining challenge trend on the Internet, teaming up with all his YouTube friends.

PointlessBlogVlogs: When he's not busy vlogging, you'll find Alfie Deyes taking on 'pointless' challenges, like waxing his underarms and covering his face with cream. He's even challenged Ariana Grande to do his makeup.

CHALLENGE INSPIRATION

111. THE DIZZY CHALLENGE

Guaranteed to make your viewers laugh, the dizzy challenge involves performing a variety of tasks while you're – you guessed it – dizzy.

Top Tips
Come up with your own spin (geddit?) on this challenge by thinking up some even sillier tasks to carry out while dizzy. Just don't do it anywhere dangerous.

Prepare
Prepare the challenge tasks and any equipment you'll need before you start filming. You'll also need an office chair to spin round on – get the sick bucket ready! Set up your camera so that it will capture the whole scene.

Film
Spin around on the chair until you're dizzy before attempting to complete the tasks without losing your balance. Tasks could include anything from an obstacle course to holding a yoga pose and even juggling eggs.

Watch
The Dizzy Challenge |
ThatcherJoe
– ThatcherJoe

☐ **Video completed**

Date ___/___/___

NOTES:...
....
....

112. TRY NOT TO LAUGH CHALLENGE

So you think you're funny? Put your wit to the test with the Try Not to Laugh Challenge, where you'll try to make your opponent, who has a mouth full of water, crack up in any way you can.

Top Tips
You can also play a version of this challenge without a friend, by watching ready-made YouTube compilations of some of the funniest clips on the Internet. See how far you can make it without laughing.

Prepare
You'll need lots of water and a sense of humour, as well as a change of clothes for this one (unless neither of you are very funny).

Film
Your opponent should take a huge sip of water, and the aim of the game is to make them laugh within 30 seconds. This usually results in them either spitting out the water all over you or themselves.

Watch
TRY NOT TO
LAUGH CHALLENGE! –
Wassabi VLOGS

☐ **Video completed**

Date ___/___/___

NOTES:...
....
....

CHALLENGE INSPIRATION

113. NOT MY ARMS CHALLENGE

The idea of this challenge is to wear a large t-shirt with someone else's arms through it, and try to get ready with their hands doing the work instead of yours. Sounds easy, right? Wrong.

Prepare
You'll need one large t-shirt and another pair of arms to borrow. Lay out all the tools you need to get ready within arm's length too.

Film
Film yourself and your friend as you 'get ready' with their arms while yours are kept behind your back. From putting makeup on, to brushing teeth and styling your hair, this is a challenge that's MUCH funnier when you fail.

Top Tips
You could also try the Not My Legs Challenge for double the fun. Take it turns using one person's legs with the other person's torso.

Watch
Not My Arms Challenge With My Brother | Zoella – Zoella

☐ **Video completed**
Date ___/___/___

NOTES:...
....
....

---

114. THE ACCENT CHALLENGE

This challenge video is a popular choice for both YouTubers and viewers, since it's easy to film and fun to watch. Put your accent abilities to the test by playing this guessing game with a friend.

Prepare
Write down different accents on some scraps of paper and put them in a hat. You can choose as many accents as you can think of, from Australian to German, Indian to Italian.

Film
Film in front of the camera as you take it in turns to pick out a piece of paper and try to talk in that accent while the other person tries to correctly guess which one it is.

Top Tips
To make the challenge tougher, get someone else who isn't playing to write down the accents for you. This way, neither of you will be able to make a lucky guess.

Watch
Accent Challenge with Marcus | 2016 Edition | Zoella – Zoella

☐ **Video completed**
Date ___/___/___

NOTES:...
....
....

CHALLENGE INSPIRATION

115. THE EGG ROULETTE CHALLENGE

If you fancy yourself lucky, try out this eggtastic challenge. Warning: this will get messy.

Prepare

To play, you'll need a box of 12 eggs. Prepare the eggs beforehand by hard-boiling 8 of the eggs and leaving 4 of them raw. Place them all back in the box once you're done, but make sure you don't know which is which.

Film

Take it in turns picking out an egg and immediately cracking it over your head (no switching it for another one). The first person to crack two raw eggs on their head loses. It may sound gross but it sure is funny to watch.

Top Tips

This would be the perfect challenge to film and upload in time for Easter. You could even paint the eggs you're using to make it extra seasonal.

Complete this video during the Easter break

Watch

EGG ROULETTE CHALLENGE – Rosanna Pansino

☐ **Video completed**

Date ___/___/___

NOTES:..
....
....

---

116. WHISPER CHALLENGE

This popular challenge involves wearing headphones and whispering. Try it out on your channel – it's a lot funnier than it sounds.

Prepare

You can play this game with two people, but the more people you have the funnier the end result will be. You'll also need a pair of headphones for each player.

Film

While the other players listen to loud music through headphones, you should whisper a phrase to one of them. They have to try and guess what the phrase is by reading your lips only, and then pass it on to the next person, with hilarious results.

Top Tips

You can use any phrases you like during the challenge, whether it's a common figure of speech, messages other popular YouTubers have used, or something totally random.

Watch

The Whisper Challenge #5 – Markiplier

☐ **Video completed**

Date ___/___/___

NOTES:..
....
....

CHALLENGE INSPIRATION

117. THE SAY ANYTHING CHALLENGE

Another popular challenge involving words, this is a great video to film with friends but be warned, if you can't think quickly enough you may end up in a very sticky situation.

Prepare
Team up with some friends to film this challenge. You just need some sticky tape and you're ready to roll.

Film
Take it in turns saying random words until someone stumbles, blanks, or repeats a word that's already been said. The other player then gets to apply a piece of sticky tape to alter their opponent's face however they want.

Top Tips
The words don't have to relate to each other at all, just have a few prepared in your head and say anything if you want to keep your face tape free.

Watch
Say Anything Challenge (ft. SUP3RFRUIT) | Tyler Oakley – Tyler Oakley

☐ **Video completed**

Date ___/___/___

NOTES:...
....
....

118. THE BLINDFOLDED MAKEUP CHALLENGE

You don't have to be a beauty guru to film this challenge. Instead of putting on perfect makeup, here the aim is to turn the tables and have it done as imperfectly as possible.

Prepare
Ask a brave friend to volunteer to take part in the challenge. You'll need a blindfold, some makeup, and probably a fair amount of makeup wipes to remove it all too.

Film
Film yourselves as you take it in turns to attempt to apply makeup products to the other person's face while wearing a blindfold. As you can imagine, the end results are often messy and always hilarious.

Top Tips
Engage with your viewers by asking them to leave a comment to let you know who they think did the best blindfolded makeup job.

Watch
DAN AND PHIL BLINDFOLDED MAKEUP CHALLENGE – Daniel Howell

☐ **Video completed**

Date ___/___/___

NOTES:...
....
....

CHALLENGE INSPIRATION

119. THE BLINDFOLDED DRAWING CHALLENGE

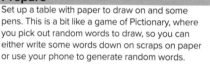

Grab a mate and show viewers your creative side by drawing pictures for the other person to guess. There's just one catch – you'll be drawing blindfolded.

Prepare
Set up a table with paper to draw on and some pens. This is a bit like a game of Pictionary, where you pick out random words to draw, so you can either write some words down on scraps on paper or use your phone to generate random words.

Film
Take it in turns to draw pictures blindfolded with the other person guessing. Set a timer to count down 30 seconds for each drawing. You get two points if the other person guesses your drawing correctly

and one point for guessing correctly – the winner is the person who is best at drawing blindfolded.

Top Tips
You can also turn this into a four-player game and compete against each other to see which team can work together to get the most correct guesses.

Watch
Blindfolded Drawing!
– Smosh 2nd Channel

☐ **Video completed**
Date ___/___/___

NOTES:..
....
....

120. YOGA CHALLENGE

If you're feeling flexible, take on this viral YouTube challenge and attempt to recreate some yoga poses with a friend.

Prepare
Look up some partner yoga moves on the Internet before filming and pick out a series of poses to copy, starting with easier ones and building up the difficulty. Next, get your sports gear on and stretch.

Film
Set up your camera to film you and your friend as you attempt to imitate some acrobatic poses, from the buddy boat to the double downward dog. Try and hold the pose for a couple of seconds, if you can, and prepare for lots of falling on the floor.

Top Tips
Make sure you insert a picture of each of the poses you're trying to copy so viewers can tell how well you did.

Watch
The Yoga Challenge!
– PointlessBlog

☐ **Video completed**
Date ___/___/___

NOTES:..
....
....

CHALLENGE INSPIRATION

121. THE SEVEN SECOND CHALLENGE

This popular challenge is heaps of fun to watch and even more fun to play. Make your own vid by completing ridiculous tasks in just seven seconds.

Prepare
You and another player will need to come up with some original and funny tasks to complete. Check out Phil Lester's original challenge for inspiration – it includes hilarious prompts such as "sing a song about bricks" and "invent a new dance".

Film
Take it in turns with a friend to give each other absurd tasks that must be completed in seven seconds or less, and just use your fingers to count down the seconds on camera. Simple.

Top Tips
There's even a '7 Second Challenge' app you can check out which has hundreds of ready-made challenge suggestions for you and your mates to have a laugh playing.

Watch
The 7 Second CHALLENGE!
(with KickThePj)
– AmazingPhil

☐ **Video completed**
Date ___/___/___

NOTES:...
....
....

122. THE TIN CAN CHALLENGE

It takes a brave person to take on the Tin Can Challenge and taste the mystery contents of cans without knowing what's inside.

Prepare
You'll need two or more people to play, but it also helps if you can enlist another person to pick out the cans for you so the contents will be a surprise. Ask them to choose a variety of different canned foods, from baked beans to tinned fish, and remove the labels before you play.

Film
Each player should take it in turns choosing and consuming the mystery contents of the unlabelled cans. Once opened, each player must eat a whole

spoonful of the contents of the tin – mmm! Get a point for each mouthful you manage to swallow.

Top Tips
It's best to use a mixture of nice and nasty tasting cans to build up the suspense and make the video more entertaining for your viewers.

Watch
The Tin Can Challenge
– PointlessBlog

☐ **Video completed**
Date ___/___/___

NOTES:...
....
....

CHALLENGE INSPIRATION

123. NO THUMBS CHALLENGE

Who needs thumbs anyway? You'll be surprised how difficult this simple sounding challenge can be when you when you battle it out with a friend in the No Thumbs Challenge.

Prepare
Both you and a friend should put tape on your hands so that you can no longer use your thumbs. Think up a set of simple tasks to compete in, such as writing your name, tying shoelaces, buttoning a shirt and opening a water bottle, and make sure you have everything you need.

Film
With your thumbs taped up, you must adapt to using just your fingers to compete against

each other in the tasks you've chosen. Whoever manages to complete the most tasks first is crowned the No Thumb champion.

Top Tips
Lots of YouTubers have already attempted this challenge, so try to think of some unique tasks to try that you haven't already seen in anyone else's video.

Watch
NO THUMBS CHALLENGE!
– TiffyQuake

☐ **Video completed**
Date ____/____/____

NOTES:...
....

124. THE BALLOON CHALLENGE

The balloon challenge is one of the latest trends to sweep through YouTube. Your audience will love to watch you take part in some balloon popping shenanigans.

Prepare
You'll need to blow up a LOT of balloons before beginning the challenge, and find a friend to take part with you.

Film
Try and pop your balloons by using different methods in a series of mini rounds. From the tummy punch to the chest bump and plain old sitting on them, the first person to pop their balloon using the least attempts in each round is the winner.

Top Tips
It's a good idea to keep on top of trends and make your own version of trending challenges when they first pop up on YouTube. This way, yours has more chance of being seen.

Watch
BALLOON CHALLENGE!!
– Jake Mitchell

☐ **Video completed**
Date ____/____/____

NOTES:...
....
....

CHALLENGE INSPIRATION

125. THE LANGUAGE CHALLENGE

People from all over the world tune in to watch YouTube videos, so why not try your hand at speaking some other languages. Who knows, play this challenge enough and you might even pick up a few new words.

Prepare
Think of a few sentences you want to say, and then pick some languages to translate them into. You'll need to use an online translator for this, unless you speak a lot of languages.

Film
Take it in turns with a friend to attempt to say your translated sentences out loud to the other player. They then have to guess which language it is as well as taking a stab at what the sentence means. Award a point for each correct guess.

Top Tips
Try to pronounce the words as best you can, but if you're really struggling with some of the languages you can always play the sentence out loud on the translator to help.

Watch
LANGUAGE CHALLENGE WITH ZOELLA
– Jim Chapman

☐ **Video completed**

Date ____/____/____

NOTES:..
....

126. BOYFRIEND DOES MY MAKEUP

An oldie but still a goodie, viewers never get bored of watching a boyfriend blunder his way through a makeup challenge.

Prepare
Let your boyfriend (or any male friend) loose on your makeup stash (and your face). Just sit back and hope for the best.

Film
Film your boyfriend attempting to apply a full makeup look to your face from start to finish. Give him all the products and tools you'd usually use, from primer to contour powder, and see how good his makeup skills are.

Top Tips
Don't give your boyfriend any instructions or guidance during the video – even if he's preparing to put lipstick on your eyelids – it'll make your video even funnier.

Watch
BOYFRIEND DOES MY MAKEUP | NikkieTutorials
– NikkieTutorials

☐ **Video completed**

Date ____/____/____

NOTES:..
....
....

CHALLENGE INSPIRATION

127. TOUCH MY BODY CHALLENGE

Think you can easily tell your elbows from your toes? In the Touch My Body challenge, it gets a whole lot harder as you have to guess the body part blindfolded!

Prepare
You'll need a blindfold, or scarf, to cover your eyes and another person to play the game with. Set up your camera to get you and your friend in shot.

Film
Take it in turns with one of you wearing the blindfold while the other person places your finger on a body part of theirs whilst you guess which part of the body it is. You get one guess only and the person with the most correct guesses wins.

Top Tips
Film this video with someone that you're close to – it could be a little bit uncomfortable otherwise.

Watch
TOUCH MY BODY CHALLENGE - w/ Joey Graceffica! – Miranda Sings

☐ **Video completed**

Date ___/___/___

NOTES:..
....
....

128. THE CHICKEN NUGGET CHALLENGE

This classic YouTube eating challenge may seem like a whole lot of fun but be warned, you might never want to see another chicken nugget again afterwards.

Prepare
You and a friend are going to need a whole lot of chicken nuggets. Get a couple of glasses of water ready too, and start the challenge on an empty stomach.

Film
The aim of the game is to eat as many chicken nuggets as you can in 20 minutes. Start a countdown clock and get chomping on camera. The winner is the player who manages to eat the most.

Top Tips
YouTube-inspired food challenges can sometimes be dangerous. Always use common sense before trying out any challenges you see online and be careful not to eat too quickly or put too much in your mouth at once.

Watch
The FINAL Chicken Nugget Challenge (2015) | Tyler Oakley – Tyler Oakley

☐ **Video completed**

Date ___/___/___

NOTES:..
....
....

CHALLENGE INSPIRATION

129. ICE BUCKET CHALLENGE

This viral challenge has been doing the rounds since 2014, when it was started to raise money for charity. Since then, everyone seems to have filmed their own, from Taylor Swift to Barack Obama. If you haven't already, here's your chance.

Prepare
Fill a bucket with ice and water and decide where to film your challenge – preferably outdoors or somewhere you don't mind getting wet.

Film
Brace yourself and ask someone to film as you pour a bucket of ice-cold water on your head, or get someone to do it for you. Afterwards, nominate a friend to take up the challenge too.

Top Tips
Since challenge videos can often quickly spread across the Internet, they're a great way to try and raise awareness and money for charities. If you have a cause that's close to your heart, you could start your own challenge for a charity of your choice.

Watch
38 Celebs Do the ALSIce Bucket Challenge #1 - Bieber, Niall Horan, Selena Gomez, Taylor Swift – Shine On Media

☐ **Video completed**

Date ____/____/____

NOTES:..
....

130. TRY NOT TO CRY CHALLENGE

Similar to the try not to laugh challenge, but much more emotional, the aim of this challenge is to watch sad videos and try your best to keep your eyes dry.

Prepare
Set up a compilation of sad videos to watch – there are loads of ready-made playlists already available on YouTube for this challenge.

Film
Set up a camera to film your facial reactions to the tear-inducing videos as you watch them. The goal is to make it through to the end without shedding a single tear.

Top Tips
You'll need to keep up a running commentary through the video to keep viewers interested – they don't want to just watch you watching videos the whole way through.

Watch
TRY NOT TO CRY CHALLENGE! – Guava Juice

☐ **Video completed**

Date ____/____/____

NOTES:..
....
....

CHALLENGE INSPIRATION

131. 100 LAYERS CHALLENGE

This popular yet bizarre challenge has been done with everything from makeup to t-shirts and tin foil, and involves putting layers and layers of stuff on your body – 100 layers, in fact.

Prepare
For this challenge you'll need to film when you have a lot of free time to spare – it could take a while. You'll also need to decide what you're going to layer up and make sure you have enough for 100 layers.

Film
Whether you're putting on 100 layers of foundation, nail polish, or socks, sit down in front of the camera and get started. You'll definitely need to cut down and speed parts of the video up during editing,

especially if you're applying something like nail polish where you need to wait for each layer to dry.

Top Tips
If you can, try to think of something that hasn't been done much yet and layer that up.

Watch
100+ Coats of Nail Polish I #POLISHMOUNTAIN – Simply Nailogical

☐ **Video completed**

Date ____/____/____

NOTES:...
....
....

---

132. COTTON BALL CHALLENGE

In this easy-to-film challenge, you have to try and get as many cotton balls into a bowl as you can while blindfolded. It's a lot harder than it sounds...

Prepare
All you need is a bowl full of cotton balls, an empty bowl, a spoon and a blindfold and you're ready to take the challenge.

Film
Hold the empty bowl on top of your head and place the bowl of cotton balls in front of you. You then have to use the spoon to try and scoop as many cotton balls into the bowl on your head while blindfolded. Guess how many you've managed to get – you'll probably be in for a surprise.

Top Tips
This challenge can be completed alone but it's also a lot of fun to film with friends. Turn it into a competition to see who can get the most cotton balls in a certain number of scoops.

Watch
COTTON BALL CHALLENGE – BFvsGF

☐ **Video completed**

Date ____/____/____

NOTES:...
....
....

CHALLENGE INSPIRATION

133. THE BRAIN FREEZE CHALLENGE

This classic challenge video is sure to keep your viewers laughing. Get a crazy friend to climb into an ice-cold tub of water and answer questions until they get one right, or just get brain freeze.

Prepare
Beg a friend to be your willing victim in any way you can and prepare a list of obscure questions to ask them. When you're ready to film, fill a bathtub with cold water and ice cubes.

Film
Get your friend to sit in the ice cube filled water and fire general knowledge questions at them. They can only get out when they answer a question correctly.

Top Tips
The point of this challenge is to make it as difficult as possible for your friend to get a question right. Freezing and frustrated makes for a very funny combination.

Watch
MyLifeAsEva - BRAIN FREEZE CHALLENGE – Caspar

☐ **Video completed**

Date ____/____/____

NOTES:...
....
....

134. EAT IT OR WEAR IT CHALLENGE

If you can stomach the thought of either eating cat food, or smearing it all over your face, then this messy roulette-type eating game is the challenge for you.

Prepare
You'll need a variety of both tasty and not-so-tasty food items, from ketchup and popcorn to canned spinach and even cat food. Assign numbers to each item, then write the numbers down on separate pieces of paper and put them into a hat.

Film
Players will take it in turns to pick a random number out of the box and find the matching food item. They then have to decide whether to eat a whole spoonful

of the contents or choose to be covered in it instead. Warning: this game can get very messy very fast.

Top Tips
It's probably a good idea not to put on your best clothes before filming this challenge. They have been known to end in an epic food fight!

Watch
EAT IT OR WEAR IT CHALLENGE! – Rclbeauty101

☐ **Video completed**

Date ____/____/____

NOTES:...
....
....

CHALLENGE INSPIRATION

135. THE SHOCK BALL CHALLENGE

Challenge yourself to a back and forth game of categories with a shocking twist.

Prepare

The game involves racking your brain for items that fit a certain topic. Choose a few category rounds to go back and forth answering with a friend, from breeds of dog to One Direction songs. Now for the twist – you'll need to get an electric shock ball.

Film

Start the first round and pass the ball between you every time a player answers correctly. If you can't think of an answer you keep holding the ball until you can, making it much more likely you'll receive the shock. Start a new round after each shock.

Top Tips

Repeating an item that has already been named is not allowed. If this happens and the ball has already left their hands, immediately chuck the ball back so they can answer again.

Watch

SHOCK BALL CHALLENGE WITH - JENNXPENN!
– Joey Graceffa

☐ **Video completed**

Date ____/____/____

NOTES:..
....
....

136. WORLD RECORD CHALLENGES

Fancy being a Guinness World Record breaker? Pick a challenge, film your attempt and compete with your mates. Even if you don't manage to break a record, viewers will love to watch you try.

Prepare

There are boatloads of record-breaking challenges to attempt, you just need to pick one that you think you might be able to achieve. Check out the rules of the record before filming.

Film

Film yourself as you compete in the challenge, whether you're trying to put on the most bangles in 30 seconds or eating eight saltine crackers in less than a minute. You'll need someone to time you.

Top Tips

These kind of fast challenges make great videos for your channel because you don't need to think up new ideas, just follow the instructions. They're also quick to film, take very little editing, and viewers love them.

Watch

BROTHERS BREAK EVEN MORE WORLD RECORDS
– Oli White

☐ **Video completed**

Date ____/____/____

NOTES:..
....
....

CHALLENGE IDEAS

Can you think of 10 more challenge videos to film? New challenges are constantly popping up on YouTube, so keep an eye out. Or, come up with your own cool new challenge idea – maybe it'll be your video that goes viral next.

137 ....

138 ....

139 ....

140 ....

141 ....

142

143

144

145

146

NOTES:

CHALLENGE NOTES

DIY & CRAFT

From Tumblr-themed room ideas to amazing art projects and one-of-a-kind clothes, YouTube DIY and craft videos have made it possible for viewers to learn how to create almost anything for their own homes. If you're crafty with a paintbrush or full of creative ideas, why not get in front of the camera and Do It Yourself?

CHANNEL INSPIRATION:

MayBaby: Whether you're looking for ideas to revamp your room or make going back to school more exciting, MayBaby's channel is sure to inspire you with a DIY project for every aspect of life.

SoCraftastic: With one of the most creative DIY channels on YouTube, Sarah makes all sorts of unique crafts that you won't see anywhere else, from cute charms to sweet treats, bath goodies and jewellery.

LaurDIY: Lauren, aka LaurDIY, is the queen of innovative fashion fix DIYs. If you're after easy and affordable tutorials to take your old outfits from boring to brand new, make this girl your go-to guru.

DIY & CRAFT INSPIRATION

147. CRAFTING TUTORIALS

Craft channels are like a treasure trove of tutorials teaching viewers how to make almost anything. If you're good with a glue gun, upload your own crafty tutorials to provide your viewers with endless DIY projects to do – they'll never be bored again.

Prepare
Think of a few crafts you'd like to make in advance and make sure you have all the materials you need. From paper crafts to cute decorations and polymer clay projects, you don't have to stick to just one kind of crafting on your channel.

Film
Whatever you decide to create, make sure your tutorial is broken down into simple steps and try to use budget friendly materials where possible.

Top Tips
Subscribe to some of the top crafting vloggers on YouTube for some channel inspiration. Pay close attention to the way they format and shoot their videos – you'll be surprised how much you can pick up just by watching other people's videos.

Watch
5-Minute Crafts To Do When You're BORED!! Quick and Easy DIY Ideas! – Cute Life Hacks

☐ **Video completed**
Date ____/____/____

NOTES:..
....

148. DIY FASHION

If you have a passion for arts and crafts and a love for clothes, teach your viewers how to stay on trend without blowing the budget with a DIY fashion tutorial.

Prepare
Raid your local craft supplies store or charity shop to find things you can use to update the old items in your wardrobe or transform them into something totally new.

Film
Film yourself as you get hands-on with your old clothes and DIY supplies. Turn an old pair of jeans into a new pair of shorts; customise a jacket by sewing on badges or even whip up your own slogan tee.

Top Tips
Usually fashion DIYers will show what their finished items look like on. Catch a viewer's attention in the first few seconds by showing them the project you're about to complete, and reassure them how easy it was to do.

Watch
DIY Bikinis & Swim Suit Makeovers for Summer! – LaurDIY

☐ **Video completed**
Date ____/____/____

NOTES:..
....
....

DIY & CRAFT INSPIRATION

149. DIY GIFTS

If you're short on cash or just fancy getting creative this Christmas, why not try out homemade gift giving – YouTube style. Share your gift-making DIYs and inspire your viewers in the process.

Prepare
Brainstorm some original DIY gift ideas to suit all of your loved ones. If you have lots of ideas, why not categorise your gift videos by person, giving viewers heaps of ideas for things to make for their mum/dad/brother/sister/best friend etc.

Film
Aim to show around five different gift ideas. Let viewers know the items they will need to make each DIY, before going through the steps and showing how you made them one by one.

Top Tips
Some DIY YouTubers make DIYs in front of the camera, and some set their camera up to film only their hands. If you want to include a mixture of both shots you'll need to have two cameras filming.

Watch
Last Minute DIY Gifts Ideas You NEED To Try! For BFF, Boyfriend, Parents... Birthdays/Christmas – DIYlover

☐ **Video completed**

Date ____/____/____

NOTES:...
....

150. DIY ROOM DÉCOR

DIY room décor videos are always super popular on YouTube. Let your inner interior designer loose and come up with some fun DIYs to spice up any space.

Prepare
Plan some DIYs that viewers can recreate to decorate their own rooms with, from cute fairy light jars to candles, nifty storage ideas, pillows, photo frames and inspiration boards.

Film
Film an easy-to-follow how-to tutorial showing viewers how you made each of your DIY items. You can also include any tips and hacks you have for storage and organisation ideas.

Top Tips
Pinterest and Tumblr-inspired room ideas are some of the most popular room DIY videos on YouTube. Make your own by scouring these sites for cool room pictures and ideas to try and recreate.

Watch
DIY Tumblr + Pinterest ROOM DECOR! | 2016 – Katherine Elizabeth

☐ **Video completed**

Date ____/____/____

NOTES:...
....
....

DIY & CRAFT INSPIRATION

151. DIY SWAP

If you have any craft items lying around that you don't know what to do with, you could swap with a friend and get something new.

Prepare
You'll need to collaborate with a fellow YouTuber for this video. Each of you should prepare a box containing seven different items for the other person. The challenge is to make a new DIY using at least five of the things you receive.

Film
Unbox the craft items you've been sent on camera and film your reactions, then create a new DIY out of them (you can use your own tools). The other person will do the same on their channel, so make sure you tell subscribers to check it out to see the things that you sent.

Top Tips
Collaborating with others in your community is a great way to get more exposure for your channel. Start networking by subscribing to other small channels and commenting on their videos.

Watch
Spring DIY Swap Challenge w/ Hannah Rupp (Unboxing) – Mademoiselle Ruta

☐ **Video completed**

Date ____/____/____

NOTES:..
....
....

---

152. SEWING DIY

Do you have serious skills with a needle and thread? If so, turn your talents into a sewing tutorial, teaching viewers how to construct all kinds of items and become their own fashion designer.

Prepare
Decide what you want to make. It could be a new top, a pillowcase or even a prom dress, depending on your sewing skills. Take measurements, make sure you have all the materials you need and get your sew on.

Film
It can be tricky to explain sewing patterns and methods so whether you're teaching the sewing basics or taking on a project, film every step of the process and make instructions as straightforward as possible.

Top Tips
It might help to write out your steps before recording a voiceover. This way, you can make sure you're giving the instructions in the most clear and concise way possible.

Watch
How to Make a Pillowcase (for Beginners!) | WITHWENDY – withwendy

☐ **Video completed**

Date ____/____/____

NOTES:..
....
....

DIY & CRAFT INSPIRATION

153. HALLOWEEN HOW-TO

You can't beat a good homemade Halloween costume. Fun to make, cheap and creative, viewers will flock to your channel for some last-minute spooky inspiration.

Prepare
Think of some cool outfit ideas to help viewers pull together the perfect Halloween look. Whether you're going for creative, creepy or cute, try to think outside the box and put your own unique spin on your costume ideas.

Film
From Snapchat filters and memes to zombie brides, unicorns and YouTubers, film a lookbook or tutorial type video showing viewers your Halloween getups and telling them how they can recreate the look at home.

Top Tips
Viewers are usually searching for quick and easy inspiration, rather than an outfit they have to make from scratch. Try to film some ideas that can either be put together from items people might already have at home or they can easily buy and craft.

Complete this video in October

Watch
30 Last-Minute DIY Halloween Costume Ideas! – CloeCouture

☐ **Video completed**

Date ___/___/___

NOTES:...
....
....

154. LIFE HACKS

Life hack videos are full of clever little tips and tricks that seem so obvious you wonder how you never knew about them before. Make a video sharing handy shortcuts with your subs – life will never be the same again.

Prepare
If you don't already know some, do some research and compile a list of life hacks to make your own video about – there are literally thousands on the Internet.

Film
Make a short video offering at least 10 useful life hacks that are sure to make viewers lives easier. From DIY tips to declutter your desk to quick phone fixes, you'll need to film a series of clips showing how each of the life hacks works in action.

Top Tips
You could base your hacks video around a theme, such as beauty or household hacks, an event, such as prom or back to school, or just cover all kinds of general life hacks – it's up to you.

Watch
50 Back To School Life Hacks Everyone Should Know!! – Wengie

☐ **Video completed**

Date ___/___/___

NOTES:...
....
....

DIY & CRAFT INSPIRATION

155. DIY TIE-DYE

DIY tie-dye videos are always trendy on YouTube – who doesn't love to wear colourful one-of-a-kind clothes? Upload your own tutorial showing viewers how to make all kinds of unique tie-dye designs.

Prepare
Choose some white items to tie-dye. To do the tie-dye, you'll need fabric dye (any colours you want) rubber bands and plastic gloves. If you've never tie-dyed before, check out some other YouTube tutorials to see how it's done.

Film
Film a tutorial as you tie-dye pretty much anything you like: t-shirts, shorts, shoes, pillowcases... the list is endless. Show viewers how to do it themselves with a step-by-step guide teaching the techniques you used to add different patterns and colours.

Top Tips
Tie-dye screams summer, so this is an ideal DIY video to film at the start of the holidays. Not only will it be the perfect summer boredom buster, but viewers can do it outside too.

Watch
FUN SUMMER TIE-DYE DIYS! – Joey Graceffa

☐ **Video completed**

Date ___/___/___

NOTES:...
....
....

156. ART TUTORIAL

If you're an artist at heart, this is the perfect video upload for you to share your skills with the world.

Prepare
Are you amazing at drawing realistic eyes, or a pro with colouring pencils? Whether it's a quick portrait, painting with watercolours or doodling cartoons, pick an art subject that you're good at to make a tutorial on.

Film
Film a how-to tutorial teaching viewers how to draw and paint like a pro. Focus the camera on your hands as you complete your work of art and offer tips and advice in a voiceover, which you can record after editing.

Top Tips
When it comes to repetitive actions like painting a solid colour or shading a large section, edit your video to only show the most important parts. You can do this by speeding these parts up or fading from the beginning of the clip to the end.

Watch
How to Draw Hair: 1 Character, 3 Styles [Narrated Tutorial] – markcrilley

☐ **Video completed**

Date ___/___/___

NOTES:...
....

DIY & CRAFT INSPIRATION

157. DIY BEAUTY PRODUCTS

DIY beauty tutorials are hugely popular on YouTube. Get in on the trend and show viewers how to save a few bucks by making their own beauty products.

Prepare
Choose a fun beauty DIY to try for yourself. The best thing about this tutorial is you can make lots of the beauty products using items you already have in your fridge.

Film
Film a DIY beauty tutorial showing viewers how to make their own products, from lip scrubs and soaps to body butter and facemasks. Include information on all of the items you used to make them.

Top Tips
Take a few 'beauty shots' of your finished DIYs to include in the thumbnail, styling the object and setting a nice scene. Good thumbnails automatically make your videos look put together and professional, making viewers much more likely to click.

Watch
DIY Baby Lips | DIY Tinted lip balm (2 Ways) – JENerationDIY

☐ **Video completed**

Date ____/____/____

NOTES:...
....
....

158. BACK TO SCHOOL DIYs

Make some cool DIY supplies that will make your viewers actually want to go back to school.

Prepare
It's surprisingly easy to make some creative back to school supplies with little money and effort. Brainstorm a few easy DIY ideas you can try, from jazzing up boring notebooks to making personalised labels, backpacks, custom book covers and crafty pens and pencils.

Film
Include around five different ideas for back to school DIYs that are sure to keep your viewers in style. Make sure you include step-by-step instructions covering the materials and methods used.

Top Tips
Whether you're talking straight to camera or recording a voiceover, don't forget to smile! Smiling makes a huge difference to the way you sound and will make viewers more excited about watching and wanting to recreate your DIYs.

Watch
DIY School Supplies You Need To Try For Back To School – MayBaby

☐ **Video completed**

Date ____/____/____

NOTES:...
....
....

DIY & CRAFT INSPIRATION

159. SPEED DRAWING

It doesn't matter if you're a brilliant artist or you struggle to hold a pencil, this arty challenge is guaranteed to be a lot of fun.

Top Tips
Take it in turns to show close-ups of your drawings to the camera at the end of each drawing round and let your viewers decide who wins.

Prepare
You'll need two or more people to take part in this video, and some paper and pens to draw with. Decide together what you want to draw before you start recording. You could choose anything from celebrities and cartoon characters to animals or random objects.

Film
Set up your camera to film a wide shot of you and your friends as you all sit at a table to draw the same picture in a short time span and see whose is best at the end. Set a timer and start drawing – you have a minute to win it.

Watch
STAR WARS SPEED DRAWING – Smosh 2nd Channel

☐ **Video completed**

Date ___/___/___

NOTES:...
....
....

160. DIY BATH BOMB

Bath bomb DIYs are big business on YouTube, with everyone wanting to know how to make their own at home. It's easy to make your own tutorial with the help of a few handy kitchen ingredients.

Top Tips
Once you have one bath bomb under your belt, you can experiment with all kinds of tutorials, from giant bath balls to different shapes, scents and every colour under the rainbow.

Prepare
All you'll need for a basic bath bomb is baking soda, salt, lemon juice, water, a spray bottle and some food colouring. Check out the galaxy bath bomb tutorial for inspo and exact measurements.

Film
Mix the ingredients together on camera and explain to your viewers what you're doing at every step. Get as creative as you like during the food colouring stage, and you can even add some fragrance if you fancy.

Watch
DIY: How To Make a GALAXY Bath Bomb! – Rclbeauty101

☐ **Video completed**

Date ___/___/___

NOTES:...
....
....

DIY & CRAFT INSPIRATION

161. CUSTOM COFFEE CUP

As well as putting your old coffee shop cups to good use, this fun DIY allows you to really let your creative side loose.

Prepare
All you'll need is a coffee cup (any size will do), a bunch of craft supplies and a lot of imagination.

Film
The aim of this DIY is to turn your old, boring coffee cup into something extraordinary. Whether you choose to make a jewel-encrusted cup, add some custom artwork or cover it with glitter, film the entire transformation process from start to finish.

Top Tips
Check out Pinterest for some coffee cup inspiration. Some cover every inch with embellishments, some cleverly incorporate the logo in their artistic designs, and some even turn their cup into something else entirely – new room decor anyone?

Watch
Drawing on my Starbucks Cup: Under The Sea Edition – Heather Rooney

☐ **Video completed**

Date ___/___/___

NOTES:...
....
....

162. PAPER CRAFTS

From intricate origami to calligraphy lessons, homemade cards, wrapping paper and decorations, there are many ways to get creative with paper.

Prepare
Decide what kind of paper craft you'd like to make. Prepare all the tools you'll need to make it and of course, make sure you have plenty of paper to hand.

Film
Walk viewers through your paper tutorial, clearly showing the techniques and products you use. It's a good idea to show close-up shots of your hands as you make the paper project, especially during any fiddly bits.

Top Tips
Paper crafts can be an excellent seasonal DIY tutorial to upload during the Christmas period. Teach viewers how to perfectly wrap a present or make their own gift tags or pretty gift bags out of paper.

Watch
DIY crafts: Paper GIFT BAG (Easy) - Innova Crafts – Innova Crafts

☐ **Video completed**

Date ___/___/___

NOTES:...
....
....

DIY & CRAFT INSPIRATION

163. THE DIY CHALLENGE

Collaborate with a friend in a DIY showdown that's sure to put your DIY skills to the test.

Prepare
Decide on a DIY you'll both make during the challenge – it should be something you can complete in a limited amount of time, such as a customised t-shirt or room décor art piece. Get your supplies ready, making sure you have enough variety to pick and choose from.

Film
Face off with a friend to make the same DIY in five minutes flat. You can use as many of the DIY supplies available to create your item. At the end of the video, ask your viewers to comment whose DIY they dig the most.

Top Tips
You could make this into an awesome DIY series and challenge every guest on your channel to a DIY challenge.

Watch
THE DIY CHALLENGE: LaurDIY VS. Alex Wassabi – LaurDIY

☐ **Video completed**
Date ___/___/___

NOTES:...
....
....

164. DIY SLIME

Who knew slime could be so popular? Super stretchy and addictive to play with, this sticky substance makes for the perfect DIY project.

Prepare
One of the easiest ways to make slime is to mix white glue with water, half a cup of liquid starch (added slowly) and food colouring. You can find lots of different recipes online – the fun part comes in customising your goo with whatever you like.

Film
Film a step-by-step tutorial for making slime, instructing viewers in the items they'll need and how to do it. Put your own twist on your gooey concoction by adding some extra ingredients... There's glitter slime, scented slime, glow-in-the-dark slime and even edible slime.

Top Tips
If you have enough materials, it's a good idea to make a test version of your project before filming to make sure it works. This also helps you run through the steps and figure out how to film it.

Watch
DIY | How to Make Slime WITHOUT Borax (Rainbow Slime!) – WhatsUpMoms

☐ **Video completed**
Date ___/___/___

NOTES:...
....
....

DIY & CRAFT INSPIRATION

165. YOUTUBE BACKDROP DIY

A YouTuber's background setting can set the whole tone of the channel, so it's super important to get it right. Help viewers get the perfect blogger backdrop with some unique and easy to make DIYs.

Prepare
Think of a few DIY ideas and personal touches that would improve anyone's background scene. Take some visual inspiration from other YouTubers whose set-ups you admire.

Film
From twinkly fairy light backdrops to colourful screens and cool wall art, share your top YouTube DIY tips and tricks in a tutorial video.

Top Tips
The best part about this video is that you get to use your new DIYs in your own filming room once you're done. Viewers will love to see the new personal touch to your background.

Watch
How To Build Your Own Home Studio | TECH TALK – Shameless Maya

☐ **Video completed**

Date ____/____/____

NOTES:..
....
....

166. DIY JEWELLERY

Making your own jewellery can seem quite intimidating but it doesn't have to be. DIY tutorials show viewers how simple it can be to create stunning jewellery styles without breaking the bank.

Prepare
Decide on a jewellery project to make. If you don't have access to tools such as pliers, or materials to make your jewellery items, you can easily get resourceful with items you have around the house.

Film
Film an easy to follow tutorial video, with close up shots and a voiceover explaining what you're doing. Your jewellery DIY could be as simple as a friendship bracelet or charm choker to more tricky designs.

Top Tips
Don't be afraid to stop filming and do something over again if you make a mistake... that's what editing is for. Or, keep your mistakes in the video and use them as a teaching tool to help others make the perfect DIY first try.

Watch
10 DIY Chokers | Easy and Cheap – CreationsToInspire

☐ **Video completed**

Date ____/____/____

NOTES:..
....
....

DIY & CRAFT INSPIRATION

167. DIY VALENTINE'S CARDS

Help viewers win their crush's heart by showing them how to make cute and creative homemade Valentine's cards.

Prepare
Think of a few different design ideas for unique Valentine's Day cards and make sure you have all the materials you need. Use anything from coloured card to stamps, stickers, stencils and embellishments.

Film
Whether funny puns or heartfelt messages, film a simple tutorial showing viewers how to recreate your Valentine's card designs at home.

Top Tips
Upload your video at least a week before Valentine's Day rolls around so viewers will see it in time. Why not make your own DIY card videos in time for other occasions too, such as Mother's Day and Father's Day?

Complete this video for Valentine's Day

Watch
Easy DIY Valentine's Day Card Made with Minimal Supplies – K Werner Design

☐ **Video completed**
Date ___/___/___

NOTES...
....
....

168. TESTING WEIRD LIFE HACKS

You've already heard of life hacks, but did you know there's a whole other kind of hacks video, all about putting some of the sillier hacks to the test.

Prepare
Scour the Internet for some of the craziest sounding DIY life hacks you can find. You'll then need the necessary materials to be able to follow the instructions and test them out for yourself.

Film
Test out some weird life hacks and DIYs in front of the camera to find out if they're brilliant or best left on the Internet. From putting potatoes on your armpits to using a toilet roll as a speaker, let viewers know if it's a hack, or if it's wack!

Top Tips
These videos are especially entertaining to watch when the life hack goes wrong. Don't forget to ask your viewers which weird life hacks they'd like to see you try out next.

Watch
TESTING DUMB PINTEREST HACKS – PsychoSoprano

☐ **Video completed**
Date ___/___/___

NOTES:..
....
....

DIY & CRAFT INSPIRATION

169. DIY POLYMER CLAY

Affordable and fun to use, this modelling material is all over YouTube. Use it to make all kinds of DIY projects, from jewellery to home décor.

Prepare
Whether you're a total beginner or a polymer pro, find a clay project or two to suit your skill level. You'll need to get your hands on some different coloured polymer clay and use an oven to bake your creation in.

Film
Make a how-to video showing viewers all the tools and techniques you used to make your unique polymer project, step-by-step, and don't forget to bake it.

Top Tips
Keep in mind when you're getting your clay that different colours can be mixed to make new colours, just like you would do with paints.

Watch
DIY Mini Unicorn - Polymer Clay Charm - How To - SoCraftastic – SoCraftastic

☐ **Video completed**

Date ____/____/____

NOTES:..
....
....

170. SCRAPBOOKING

Did you know there's such a thing as National Scrapbooking Day? Well, there is – every year on the first Saturday of May. If you're looking for a fun project to share with your subscribers, this is the perfect time to start scrapping!

Prepare
Scrapbooks are personal memory-keeping projects for preserving photos, mementos, family history, stories and other memorabilia. Look over some of your own treasured snaps and mementos to make your own album with, and start planning your first page layout.

Film
Film your scrapbooking tutorial from above as you show viewers how you go about creating your layouts, sharing your scrapbook kit, tips and

techniques. Get creative with patterned paper, paints, stamps, decorative lettering, embellishments and journaling.

Top Tips
Provide viewers with endless scrapbooking inspiration by turning this DIY into a series of videos sharing your scrapbook process – one page at a time.

Watch
Happy National Scrapbook Day! – Amy Tangerine

☐ **Video completed**

Date ____/____/____

NOTES:..
....

DIY & CRAFT INSPIRATION

171. DIY CANDLES

Because they're easy to make, look good in any room and make for the perfect presents. You just can't beat a good candle.

Prepare
Pick a candle DIY to make yourself. From 'no wax' candles to candles made from crayons, there are lots of easy recipe options available online.

Film
Make your own candle tutorial in any shape, size, scent or container you want – the more creative the better.

Watch
DIY Cupcake Candle // Candle Making How To – SoCraftastic

☐ **Video completed**

Date ___ / ___ / ___

172. DIY LIFE SKILLS

Do you know how to change a tyre or the easiest way to tie a tie? Many people don't – teach them how.

Prepare
Make a list of smart life hacks and skills that you can share with your viewers.

Film
From survival skills that could save a life to household hacks solving everyday problems, break your how-to tips down into easy to follow steps, with video clips to match.

Watch
How to Change a Flat Tire! (Smart Life Hacks w/ Kerri Doherty) – Amy Poehler's Smart Girls

☐ **Video completed**

Date ___ / ___ / ___

173. CREATIVE JOURNAL

Creative journaling is the latest DIY planning trend. If you love nothing more than making to-do lists, then this is the DIY for you.

Prepare
A cross between a to-do list and a diary, this popular system can seem a little confusing at first, so do your research and watch a few tutorials before getting started. Then all you need is a journal and a pen...

Film
Make your own tutorial video teaching viewers how to create their own journal and share your ideas and top tips for keeping organised.

Watch
BULLET JOURNAL: WHAT AND HOW?! I Lily Pebbles – Lily Pebbles

☐ **Video completed**

Date ___ / ___ / ___

DIY & CRAFT IDEAS

Add 10 more ideas for awesome DIYs to do. From clothes customisations to DIY phone cases and unique gifts, there are endless ways to get of creative with crafts.

174

175

176

177

178

179 ....
....
....
....

180 ....
....
....
....

181 ....
....
....
....

182 ....
....
....
....

183 ....
....
....
....

NOTES: ....
....
....
....

DIY & CRAFT NOTES

TRAVEL

Packed full of planet Earth eye candy, culture, storytelling, travel vlogs and an endless supply of info, YouTube travel videos are the first place viewers look to get inspiration for their next adventure. If you've always dreamt of travelling the world, take your video camera, vlog your adventures and turn your passion into an online following.

CHANNEL INSPIRATION:

vagabrothers: Marko and Alex are backpacking brothers on a mission to explore the world and share the stories of the people who live in it. Check them out for entertaining, educational travel videos packed with culture.

Hey Nadine: Want to know how you can travel the world? Nadine's awesome channel has all the inspiration, knowledge and advice you need to make your wanderlust dreams come true.

FunForLouis: Creating daily vlogs from every far-flung corner of the globe, this modern day explorer makes every day an adventure and loves to inspire his followers to get outside, explore and enjoy life.

TRAVEL INSPIRATION

184. TRAVEL VIDEOS

If you're going to start making travel videos, vlogging is the very best thing you can do to show viewers the world from your point of view.

Prepare

All you really need is a camera and a sense of adventure, but it doesn't hurt to watch other travel vloggers first to help you find your own style. Travel vlogger, RayaWasHere, says she learnt everything she knows about filming and editing by watching other people's videos.

Film

Get your camera out as often as you can on your travels to take viewers around the globe with you. Give a sense of the place through glimpses into your daily activities, experiences and thoughts, both in front of and behind the camera.

Top Tips

The magic of travel vlogs comes in editing them well, and you'll likely have a lot of footage you need to cut down. Use short clips to keep the video's pace fast and exciting. Stunning shots of scenery are all well and good, but every shot should add up to tell the story of your trip.

Watch
LIVING THE ADVENTURE
– FunForLouis

☐ **Video completed**
Date ___/____/____

NOTES:...
....
....

185. GAP YEAR SERIES

Going on a gap year? Take this opportunity to document your travels. Not only can you share your adventures with everyone at home, you might find some new friends come along for the ride.

Prepare

Decide what direction you want your gap year videos to take. You could film your adventures through daily vlogs, make videos centred around each place or activity, or offer travel tips to others.

Film

Whether you're backpacking, volunteering or working abroad, turn your adventures into a series of videos for viewers to follow along with you. You could help others who are thinking of going on a gap year too by sharing your tips for first time travels, from what to pack to where to go.

Top Tips

If you're not yet old enough to plan a gap year or save enough money, start by filming your family holidays or day trips with friends. Brush up your filming and editing skills and you'll hit the ground running.

Watch
Travel Tips - Planning your backpacking adventure
– Backpacking Bananas

☐ **Video completed**
Date ___/____/____

NOTES:...
....
....

TRAVEL INSPIRATION

186. TRAVEL ADVICE

There are lots of things to do and think about before even setting off on a trip. Luckily, there are also lots of YouTube channels dedicated to giving viewers all the practical advice they need to know – why not be one of them?

Prepare
Think of a useful travel topic, and make sure you know your stuff. From tips on saving up for travel, to booking accommodation, applying for visas and exchanging cash, there are enough pre-travel topics to turn into a whole tips series.

Film
Travel tips videos are great to film in-between travels because you don't need to leave the house to film them. Simply offer informative, in-depth advice on your chosen subject.

Top Tips
Help your channel stand out by finding a niche and focusing on that. Do you want to be known as a travel expert? A budget traveller? An entertaining travel vlogger? Of course, you're free to change up your content at any time.

Watch
20 THINGS TO DO BEFORE YOU GO TRAVELLING!!! – PsychoTraveller

☐ **Video completed**
Date ____/____/____

NOTES:...
....

187. TOP 10 THINGS TO DO

When visiting a new destination, lots of people look to YouTube first for top tips on the best things to see and do there. Give your viewers what they want with your own top 10 to-do lists.

Prepare
Whether it's a far-flung city you're visiting or your own hometown, choose your destination and write a well-researched list of 10 interesting things to do there before filming. It'll help you better explore the place too.

Film
The best way to give viewers a taste of the place is by visiting and filming the locations or activities on your list. Think of yourself as an informal travel presenter, showcasing the destinations, offering a review, advice and other essential information.

Top Tips
The most common travel searches on YouTube focus on destination names, attractions and points of interest. Make sure you include the destination name in the title of your video and use effective tags for maximum views.

Watch
Top 10 Things to DO in FLORIDA! – High On Life

☐ **Video completed**
Date ____/____/____

NOTES:...
....
....

TRAVEL INSPIRATION

188. EXTREME ACTIVITIES

Some creators like to take a trip on the wilder side, with travel videos full of adrenaline pumping activities, adventure and fun. Warning: these videos are not for the faint of heart.

Prepare
Extreme travel vloggers go to any length to showcase the exciting side of the destinations they visit. Find an unusual or exciting activity to take part in next time you visit somewhere new, if you dare.

Film
Inspire viewers to live life to the max with thrilling activities like zip lining, paragliding, rock climbing, even swimming with sharks. A first person view of the adrenaline activity makes for some great vicarious viewing – many vloggers will use something like a GoPro to achieve these shots.

Top Tips
Always stay safe when taking part in extreme sports – make sure you are wearing all the correct gear, do your research and choose to go with a reputable company. Never do anything dangerous just for a cool shot.

Watch
FREE DIVING WITH SHARKS – Mr Ben Brown

☐ **Video completed**

Date ___/___/___

NOTES:..
....
....

189. SOLO TRAVEL TIPS

If you've been lucky (and brave) enough to travel around the world on your own, make your own videos sharing your tips and advice to show viewers that they can do the same.

Prepare
Going travelling alone can be a very daunting thing to do, so write down some tips and advice that you think would be useful and reassuring to others.

Film
Film a video in front of the camera to share your honest experiences with viewers, including the benefits of solo travelling, as well as the pitfalls. Share informative tips, from packing light (there's only one person to carry it), to picking a hostel, problem solving, safety and even how to take solo travel selfies.

Top Tips
The point is to inspire others to take their own leap of faith, so try to be passionate and genuinely excited about whatever you have to say.

Watch
What's it like to Travel Solo? – Brooke Saward

☐ **Video completed**

Date ___/___/___

NOTES:..
....
....

TRAVEL INSPIRATION

190. WHAT TO PACK

An unwelcome yet essential part of any holiday – help take the stress out of luggage packing with a useful video teaching viewers what to pack for whatever the trip.

Prepare

Decide what kind of packing tutorial to make, whether it's packing hacks for a short break or tips for long-term travel. Then make your own list of essential items to take and how-to pack tips.

Film

Show viewers how to pack like a pro by using your own bag to demonstrate. Share useful tips and techniques, from rolling clothes to save space to taking travel sized everything, important items to have and even advice on the luggage itself.

Top Tips

Plan your video thoroughly beforehand, so you can make sure you have every item you need to hand. This will not only make your video quicker to shoot, it'll save time during editing too.

Watch

Travel Tips: How to Pack for Long Trips – soniastravels

☐ **Video completed**

Date ____/____/____

NOTES:...
....
....

---

191. TRAVEL STORIES

Viewers love to listen to and be inspired by real-life travelling stories. If you've got an interesting travel story to tell, now's the time to share it.

Prepare

It might help to write your story out in full. Not only will you to be able to tell it more fluently when it comes to filming, but the writing process will also help jog your memory and remember things you might have forgotten otherwise.

Film

From simply sitting in front of the camera and speaking, to overlaying photos and video clips and even dressing up and acting it out, tell your story in any way you like – so long as it's engaging.

Top Tips

Whether it's the story of your first holiday, happiest travel memory or an embarrassing encounter, story telling helps viewers connect with you on a more personal level, so let your personality shine through.

Watch

Pooping on an Indian Bus – Kristen Sarah

☐ **Video completed**

Date ____/____/____

NOTES:...
....
....

TRAVEL INSPIRATION

192. TRAVEL BUDGET TIPS

Since most of us don't have an unlimited budget to see the world with, videos all about budgeting are a popular watch for many soon-to-be travellers.

Prepare
Do some research online or use your own experiences to make a list of useful tips teaching viewers how to budget for an upcoming trip before they go.

Film
Budgeting can be confusing. From ways to save money on accommodation, transportation and food to allowing for spur of the moment activities, emergencies and hidden expenses, your video should teach viewers the basics of travelling on a tight budget and how to do it.

Top Tips
Provide links and information on any travel websites or companies you've found useful for planning trips, booking accommodation or finding cheap airfares.

Watch
TOP 10 TIPS FOR BUDGET TRAVEL – Backpacking Bananas

☐ **Video completed**

Date ___/___/___

NOTES:..
....
....

---

193. TRAVEL WISH LIST

Here's another travel video you can make without even leaving your bedroom. Share your travel wish list of the places you want to go and update viewers on your plans for the future.

Prepare
Write a list of all the places in the world you'd love to visit. It doesn't matter how near or far, realistic or exotic – this is your wish list.

Film
Film a chatty video, talking through each of the places on your wish list and the reasons why you want to visit them. Who knows, you might inspire someone else to add your picks to their wish list too.

Top Tips
This is a good video idea to make at the start of the New Year. Let viewers know about any exciting trips you have planned and what they can expect to see from your channel in the year ahead.

Watch
TRAVEL WISHLIST 2017 – BACKPACKING BRITS

☐ **Video completed**

Date ___/___/___

NOTES:..
....
....

TRAVEL INSPIRATION

194. LANGUAGE TUTORIALS

Do you speak any foreign languages? Want to learn? Share your lingo learning tips with viewers to help lessen the language barrier while travelling.

Prepare
Prepare your first lesson in teaching your chosen language. Make sure you know a few basic words and phrases that would be useful to know.

Film
It always reflects well if you at least make an effort to use the local language while travelling. Make a tutorial teaching some simple words to help viewers out, from "please" and "thank you" to common sentences, such as introducing yourself or asking for directions.

Top Tips
If you don't know another language you could always make a video sharing tips on how to overcome the barriers if you don't speak the language where you're going.

Watch
GERMAN // Basic Words + Phrases for Travelers – Mari Johnson

☐ **Video completed**

Date ___/___/___

NOTES:..
....
....

195. WHAT'S IN MY CARRY-ON?

What are the essential items that you must have on a long haul flight? Share your top tips for what to carry in your carry-on.

Prepare
Get your carry-on case ready before you start filming (or plan to film before an upcoming trip), packing it full of all the items you'd usually want to take with you on a flight.

Film
Make a What's in My Bag? style video, talking through each of the items in your travel case and explaining the reasons why they're in there, from your in-flight essentials to things you'll need when you land.

Top Tips
Keep in mind that airlines usually have weight and size restrictions for carry-on luggage, so it could also be useful to offer your tips and hacks to be able to pack as much as possible.

Watch
What's In My Travel Bag | In Flight Essentials! – Tess Christine

☐ **Video completed**

Date ___/___/___

NOTES:..
....
....

TRAVEL INSPIRATION

196. ROAD TRIP

There are all kinds of travel videos with a focus on road tripping, showing that you don't have to get on a plane or go too far to have fun.

Prepare
Decide what kind of road trip video to make. You could share some tips about how to prepare for or plan the perfect road trip, or go on an epic road trip with friends and vlog the adventure.

Film
If you decide to take your own road trip then assemble your squad, make sure your camera has enough battery life and hit the road. As well as capturing the scenery, don't forget to turn the camera on yourselves and share the adventure both inside of and outside the car.

Top Tips
Background music can make or break a travel video, so pick some good tunes that accentuate the mood of your video and the feelings you want to convey, whether that's upbeat and exciting or more chilled out vibes.

Watch
ROAD TRIP WITH MY KID OWEN! – CaseyNeistat

☐ **Video completed**

Date ___/____/____

NOTES:...
....
....

---

197. TRAVEL HACKS

Share the top hacks you've picked up on your travels to help your viewers travel further, better and cheaper than before.

Prepare
Write a list of at least 10 top travel hacks that are sure to save time, space or money on the road, from tips on how to get your baggage back first and swinging hotel discounts to storing cables without tangling and space-saving packing.

Film
You won't need any travel footage for this one, just get in front of the camera to share your top tips, tricks and hacks that every savvy traveller should know. Discuss how to do each one and show any items viewers will need.

Top Tips
For even more video ideas, try breaking your travel hacks into different categories and film a video focusing on each one. For example, you could do hair and beauty travel hacks, packing hacks or money saving hacks.

Watch
13 Travel Hacks You Need To Know | Tenani – Tenani

☐ **Video completed**

Date ___/____/____

NOTES:...
....
....

TRAVEL INSPIRATION

198. 360-DEGREE VIEWING

Provide the ultimate travel inspiration with a video showing off your destination from every angle.

Prepare
360-degree cameras that let you look in every direction are one of hottest new travel accessories. These videos obviously aren't for the beginner travel vlogger as cameras can be expensive, but if you can get your hands on one it'll make for a super cool view.

Film
Virtual reality videos let viewers navigate through the video themselves and feel like they're actually there, seeing what you see. It's best to film unique experiences and things people might not be able to see otherwise, from a helicopter ride over mountains to beautiful faraway beaches.

Top Tips
If you can't get your hands on this technology, you can still use the principal in your own videos to give viewers a better viewing experience. Show things from different angles and pan the camera around for a better perspective.

Watch
EPIC HELICOPTER 360 VIDEO – FunForLouis

☐ **Video completed**

Date ____/____/____

NOTES:..
....
....

199. CULTURE

Next time you're travelling, get off the beaten path to explore the culture of a country in more depth and educate viewers on another part of the world. You never know what you might discover.

Prepare
When exploring your destination, try to steer clear of the popular tourist destinations and look for things to do that haven't been covered so much. Do as the locals do, ask them for tips and create your own guide based on their recommendations.

Film
A unique perspective is sure to make your travel video stand out. Share the sights, sounds and smells of the place you're in, learn about the history and customs, film the local food, meet the real people who live there and share their stories.

Top Tips
Though it's usually a good idea to include background music, sometimes in travel videos it's best to let the natural background sounds take centre stage, adding to the atmosphere of your video. Just don't forget to add a wind muffler to your camera's microphone if it's windy.

Watch
GALWAY IRELAND - GAELIC TRADITIONS & CUSTOMS – vagabrothers

☐ **Video completed**

Date ____/____/____

NOTES:..
....

TRAVEL INSPIRATION

200. FAVOURITE PLACES I'VE BEEN

Share your most treasured travel memories and provide travel inspiration for others looking for some amazing destinations to visit.

Prepare
Look through your old travel footage and photos, pick a few destinations you've visited that you really loved and think through what you want to say about them.

Film
Talk about your favourite destinations: why you liked them so much and your favourite memories there. Overlaying some footage from each place while you talk will make your video more interesting and give viewers a sense of the place.

Top Tips
You definitely need to have first-hand knowledge of the places you're talking about to make this kind of video. If you've already visited the places you mention but forgot to get video footage, insert photos with a voiceover instead.

Watch
Places I have been to – Marzia

☐ **Video completed**

Date ___/___/___

NOTES:...
....
....

201. GUESS THE FLAG CHALLENGE

This is a fun game to play with friends to see how well you really know the world. Well, the flags of the world, anyway.

Prepare
Ask someone who isn't playing the game to be the quizmaster and to prepare some pictures of flags ready for the game. They can ramp up the difficulty by choosing similar looking flags.

Film
The quizmaster will name a country and show players pictures of two different flags. Players must correctly identify which of the flags belongs to that country. Award a point for each correct answer – the player who can guess the most flags wins.

Top Tips
You can also make a solo version of this video by taking an online quiz and filming the screen as you answer.

Watch
ULTIMATE Travel Vlogger FLAG CHALLENGE – Hey Nadine

☐ **Video completed**

Date ___/___/___

NOTES:...
....
....

TRAVEL INSPIRATION

202. STAYCATION

There's no rule that says you have to go far from home in order to travel. Make a video showing off the attractions of your hometown – it'll seem exotic to someone somewhere in the world.

Prepare
Search online for some fun activities, events or things to see in your area and get out there. You could visit parks or museums, check out the top attractions or take a bus to a nearby city.

Film
Vlog your adventures and make a travel guide documenting the sights you visit. Viewers who have never been before will be interested to see what there is to do there. Try to offer helpful insider tips, such as the best places to stay and which restaurants to eat at.

Top Tips
Covering a staycation might not seem like the most exciting idea to you, but you never know what other people might find interesting. The next time someone searches for your hometown, you could be their go-to guide.

Watch
Exploring Downtown LA | Shaycation Staycation – Shay Mitchell

☐ **Video completed**
Date ___/___/___

NOTES:..
....
....

203. BUCKET LIST ADVENTURES

Are you feeling adventurous? Get out there and make some of your crazy bucket list dreams come true – just don't forget to film it.

Prepare
Whether it's volunteering in another country, exploring the Galapagos Islands, swimming with whale sharks or doing a bungee jump, write down your bucket list of adventures you want to experience during your lifetime.

Film
Document and share the adventures of your bucket list items as you experience each one. This would make an exciting video series for viewers to follow along with as you check off each goal one

by one. Always try to keep your camera stable no matter what the activity – you don't want to give your viewers motion sickness at home.

Top Tips
If you're not in a position to carry out any of your bucket list dreams just yet, don't worry – you can still make a video talking through your bucket list and telling viewers why each item is on there.

Watch
My Bucket List – JacksGap

☐ **Video completed**
Date ___/___/___

NOTES:..
....

TRAVEL INSPIRATION

204. TRAVEL WITH FRIENDS

Part of the joy of travel is meeting new friends. Why not include them in your travel video for even more entertainment.

Prepare
Vlogs always become more interesting when other people get involved. You can include your travel buddies, connect with other travellers on your trip or meet up with other budding travel vloggers.

Film
Go on an outing with your friends and vlog the adventure, whether you're going on a grand adventure or just taking a trip to the next town. Viewers love to watch aspirational videos of vloggers travelling the world and having fun with friends.

Top Tips
Instead of just pointing the camera in your friends' faces, ask them a question – like what they're up to or what they think of the place you're in. This will be much more engaging and add more personality to your video.

Watch
The Best Day Ever in Venice Beach California!! – RayaWasHere

☐ **Video completed**

Date ____/____/____

NOTES:..
....
....

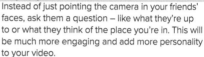

205. AIRPORT & FLIGHT ADVICE

If you're a seasoned jetsetter, share your top tips teaching others how to have a smooth journey.

Prepare
Research and write down your best advice for navigating airports and planes, from how to sleep on a plane and get the best seats to tips for nervous fliers, booking cheap flights, catching connections and what to do in case of cancellations.

Film
Simply film yourself in front of the camera as you offer your top tips and advice on how to have a good flight experience. Don't forget to include links to any websites or companies you mention.

Top Tips
Your travel advice videos should be well-researched and authentic. Insider, actual tried and tested travel knowledge is what makes good travel vloggers stand out above the crowd of information out there.

Watch
7 Weird Ways to Sleep On A Plane - Travel Tip – How 2 Travelers

☐ **Video completed**

Date ____/____/____

NOTES:..
....
....

TRAVEL INSPIRATION

206. THE TRAVEL TAG

The Travel Tag offers the perfect excuse to talk about your favourite places to go, future travel plans, give tips and generally share your love of travelling with the world.

Prepare
Find a list of the 30 Travel Tag questions on the Internet. Some of the questions require you to recall memories or places you've been to so it will definitely help to make a few notes or at least think through your answers before filming.

Film
Sit down in front of your camera to make a Q&A style video, answering each of the Travel Tag questions, such as 'Where are you from in the world?', 'How many countries have you visited?' and 'Why do you travel?'.

Top Tips
Add images and footage from your travels alongside your answers and make sure to point your viewers towards any other videos you mention during the tag.

Watch
Travel The World! | Travel Tag – MakeUpByCamila2

☐ **Video completed**
Date ____/____/____

NOTES:...
....
....

207. SAFETY TIPS

Don't want your viewers to get stranded in a foreign land with no money, no passport and no phone? Tell them how to travel safely!

Prepare
Gather up the items you think should be part of travel safety 101 to use as visual aids in your video. Items could include: a sturdy lock for your suitcase, a bumbag, a copy of your travel documents, or an item of clothing appropriate to a country you'll be travelling in.

Film
Some might think safety is boring, but that doesn't mean your video has to be. While being safe overseas is serious, you can also have a bit of fun while talking viewers through your tips – throw in a joke and smile often.

Top Tips
Do your homework before making your video to tell viewers the absolute essentials of staying safe overseas. Recommended are: not walking alone at night, not storing all your cash or cards in one place, and knowing the cultural rules of a place and any social taboos before you go.

Watch
Travel Tips: Safety First – soniastravels

☐ **Video completed**
Date ____/____/____

NOTES:...
....
....

TRAVEL INSPIRATION

208. HOW TO...

Travel vloggers seem to have the dream job. As you'd expect, one of the most common questions they get asked by viewers is, 'How do I get to do what you do?' Why not share your answer?

Prepare
Think of some tips you can share that helped you when you first started travel vlogging, or things you've learned since. You'll probably want to save this video idea until your channel is at the stage where subscribers are asking you questions.

Film
Let viewers know how you got started making travel content and how they could do the same. Tips could range from the equipment they'll need, to how to get the best shots, lighting and sound advice and even how to start making money.

Top Tips
Be honest and share your own experience and journey on YouTube, including the ups as well as the downs and any struggles you've faced.

Watch
How to Start a Travel YouTube Channel and Make Money While Traveling — Erik Conover Interview – Video Influencers

☐ **Video completed   Date __/__/__**

NOTES:...
....
....

209. TRAVEL MONTAGE

Travel montages are made up of lots of short clips to make one awesome video. These are also one of the most likely types of travel video to go viral.

Prepare
Think of a unique and fun video idea or theme for your own travel montage. Examples of already popular videos include going on an epic adventure and taking selfies everywhere you go or continuing a dance routine from one place to the next.

Film
Whatever you decide to do, you'll need to film a short clip in each place you travel to. Set up your camera the same each time so you can edit the lot together when you return. For an easier to make montage, consider turning your year of travels into one montage, with clips of your best moments.

Top Tips
This kind of video can take months or even years to gather enough short clips to make a truly great montage. The result will be worth it though if it's sharable enough to go viral.

Watch
Around the World in 360° Degrees - 3 Year Epic Selfie – Alex Chacon

☐ **Video completed Date ___/___/___**

NOTES:...
....
....

TRAVEL IDEAS

Think of 10 adventurous ideas for your own travel videos. If you've recently stayed somewhere you could make a review of it, share your biggest travel mistakes with viewers or vlog your summer getaway.

210
....
....
....
....

211
....
....
....
....

212
....
....
....
....

213
....
....
....
....

214
....
....
....
....

215

216

217

218

219

NOTES:

TRAVEL NOTES

COMEDY

Comedy is one of the most popular categories on YouTube. With channels full of parodies, pranks, sketches and silliness, YouTube comedians are the first port of call for anyone in need of a good laugh. If you've got a gift for making people giggle then get your antics on the Internet – it's your turn to be the next comedy star.

LOL

CHANNEL INSPIRATION:

Smosh: Thanks to their hilarious mix of scripted sketches, video-game themed music videos, movie spoofs and a whole lot of silliness, Smosh have one of the most subscribed channels on YouTube.

Dan & Phil: Dan and Phil have conquered YouTube together with their unique brand of quirky comedy. Check them out for awkward stories about real-life encounters, hilarious comedy skits, inventive challenges and random musings.

IISuperwomanII: Comedian, vlogger, rapper, actress... The super talented Lilly Singh can do it all. She's especially good at putting a funny spin on common issues we all face, from parent troubles to social media stresses.

COMEDY INSPIRATION

220. SKITS

Short, humorous little comedy scenes, skits are just as entertaining to make as they are to watch. Why not start off your comedy career with a skit?

Prepare
Think about what kind of skit you want to do and come up with an idea, whether it's parody, satire, relatable or completely absurd. Gather inspiration by watching other comedy skits on YouTube.

Film
The great thing about a skit is that you can film it on your own or with friends. Keep it short – skits are usually based around a single joke, and are often improvised so just wing it and ad-lib if you don't fancy writing a whole script just yet.

Top Tips
This is a great way to learn what style of comedy works for you and what doesn't. Don't be afraid to fail – your videos probably aren't going to be perfect from day one – nobody's are. Make as many mistakes as possible in your first few videos and learn from them.

Watch
Smosh - The Best Car EVER – Smosh

☐ **Video completed**

Date ___/___/___

NOTES: ....
....
....

221. SKETCH COMEDY

Sketches are among the most popular YouTube comedy videos. If you're an aspiring filmmaker with a wicked sense of humour, write out a script and turn it into a short film.

Prepare
Sketches differ to skits in that they are usually scripted, with a cast of characters. Come up with your own idea for a funny sketch. You could draw inspiration from real life situations and people. You'll then need to write your own short script.

Film
Get a group of friends together to play the characters, or you could even try your hand at acting out the different parts yourself. There's lots of opportunity for goofing around. Use props and costumes to make your comedy come to life.

Top Tips
Sound quality is super important – viewers can't laugh at your awesome lines if they can't hear them. Wherever your scenes are set, try to avoid filming anywhere with a lot of noise in the background and film a test clip to check.

Watch
YOUR GRAMMAR SUCKS #40: SKETCH – jacksfilms

☐ **Video completed**

Date ___/___/___

NOTES: ....
....
....

COMEDY INSPIRATION

222. RANT

Has something been bothering you? Get it off your chest YouTube-style in the form of a witty rant we can all relate to.

Prepare
Pick a topic to 'rant' about – the more relatable the better! You could choose to put a humorous spin on frustrating aspects of everyday life that lots of people encounter, from nosy neighbours to annoying people on public transport.

Film
Sit in front of the camera to talk about your chosen topic, whether it's poking fun at everyday situations or highlighting important issues. Some ranting YouTubers get extremely animated, some are deadpan or sarcastic, but use whatever style comes naturally to you.

Top Tips
Bear in mind that while some people love this type of video, other people might not. Say what's on your mind but be careful not to take it too far or be offensive.

Watch
I Rant For You
– JennaMarbles

☐ **Video completed**

Date ____/____/____

NOTES:...
....
....

223. IMPRESSIONS

Are you known for your amazing impressions? If you can imitate someone to perfection, make a video showing off your skills.

Prepare
Pick a few people who you think you can mimic well and brush up on your impersonation skills. It doesn't have to be limited to people – you could choose to copy anything from cartoon characters to animals.

Film
Get in front of the camera and do your best impressions one after the other, from TV characters to singers or other YouTubers. The more impersonations you can manage to fit into one short video, the more impressive it will be.

Top Tips
To make your video a little different you could combine your impressions with doing something else, such as singing a song or doing a skit.

Watch
75 IMPRESSIONS IN 5 MINUTES! – ThatcherJoe

☐ **Video completed**

Date ____/____/____

NOTES:...
....
....

COMEDY INSPIRATION

224. SLAPSTICK

Who doesn't enjoy some good old-fashioned silliness every now and then? That's what slapstick comedy's all about. From slipping and tripping over to rough-and-tumble, dropping things and spilling stuff – the opportunities to mess about are endless.

Prepare
Preparation is key to make sure your slapstick bit is going to work, and is going to at least get a few laughs. Whatever idea you have in mind, make sure you have any props that you need and have a practice run before you press record.

Film
You may want to start the video by giving viewers some context about what's to come. After that you'll need to set up a remote camera to film whatever deed or misdeed we're about to see.

Make sure the whole bit is captured in the frame – you probably won't want to redo it.

Top Tips
Don't put yourself in any danger. There's plenty you can do slapstick-wise that won't see you end up with bruises — or worse, broken bones.

Watch
Falling With Paige Ginn In Public – Danny Duncan

☐ **Video completed**
Date ____/____/____

NOTES:...
....
....

225. ROAST YOURSELF CHALLENGE

As the name suggests, this video trend offers you the chance to make a diss track all about... you! Lovingly poke a bit of fun at yourself online, if you think you're up to the challenge.

Prepare
It can be all too easy to make fun of other people, but here the goal is to turn the insults on yourself. Take a look at yourself as if you're another person and come up with a hilarious, self-deprecating rap about yourself.

Film
All you need to do is film yourself performing your 'roast' in rap or song form. You could poke fun at your own appearance, personality traits or things

you do in your YouTube videos. It definitely pays to have a sense of humour about yourself here.

Top Tips
There are many different ways you could roast yourself – try to come up with something creative, whether it's a vlog, creating a character to have a rap battle with or getting some friends involved.

Watch
Roast Yourself Challenge! – nigahiga

☐ **Video completed**
Date ____/____/____

NOTES:...
....

COMEDY INSPIRATION

226. ALTER EGOS

Some comedians carry out hilarious antics under the guise of their own original characters. Breathe new life into your channel by making your own alter ego the star for a day.

Prepare
Brainstorm some ideas for funny fictional characters to play. Who are they? What kinds of things would they say? Do they have a catchphrase? You'll then need a costume to complete the character transformation.

Film
Play the role of your character in front of the camera. You could vlog as them, act out a skit or have them interact with another person. The best thing is, your character can say and do things you wouldn't normally dream of doing.

Top Tips
Some YouTube comedians create a whole host of distinct characters, who appear so frequently we get to know them almost as well as the stars behind them. Just think – with multiple characters, the opportunities for comedy are endless.

Watch
How To Stop Parents from Comparing Kids (ft. Miranda Sings) – IISuperwomanII

☐ **Video completed**
Date ____/____/____

NOTES:..
....
....

227. EXPECTATIONS VS. REALITY

As we've all experienced, sometimes the realities of life don't quite live up to our expectations. Make your own version of this video, proving there can be a funny side when things don't go to plan.

Prepare
Think of your own video idea, perhaps drawing from something that's happened in your own life. Plan out how to film your video, from which scenes you want to act out to any props you'll need.

Film
You'll need to film a series of clips pointing out the funny differences between your expectations of a thing or an event and the reality of the situation. Edit them together creatively – you could either do

a side-by-side comparison with the clips playing at the same time or one after the other.

Top Tips
Popular examples of this video are often based around events, such as back to school, prom, sleepovers, Valentine's Day and Christmas.

Watch
Back to School: Expectations Vs Reality – MamaMiaMakeup

☐ **Video completed**
Date ____/____/____

NOTES:..
....

COMEDY INSPIRATION

228. PARODIES

Parody videos imitate and put an amusing spin on anything in popular culture, from music and movies to video games and adverts.

Prepare

Pick something to base your own parody video around, whether that's a scene from a famous movie, a film trailer or a current song. Come up with a way to put a comedy spin on it and either write out a script or some new lyrics.

Film

Whether you choose to recreate scenes from a movie or make your own version of a music video, make sure you poke plenty of fun at whatever it is you're imitating. Just keep in mind that your parody has to be different enough from the original to avoid any copyright issues.

Top Tips

Choose iconic or very well known movies, songs and scenes that viewers will instantly recognise, no matter how out there your version of it is.

Watch
Ed Sheeran - "Shape of You" PARODY – Bart Baker

☐ **Video completed**

Date ___/___/___

NOTES:..
....
....

229. BLOOPERS

Bloopers are one of the easiest comedy videos you can make, and luckily for you, viewers love to watch them too.

Prepare

This one takes very little preparation to make. Just go about filming your usual YouTube video content and keep the camera rolling during those times when you happen to make a mistake.

Film

Whether you're cracking up on camera, stumbling over your words, falling over or just being a bit weird, edit together a blooper reel consisting of all the funny moments where you've messed up during filming.

Top Tips

Blooper videos go to show you should never be afraid to make mistakes when you're making videos. Even if you're not specifically making comedy videos, bloopers can be inserted at the end of a video to keep viewers entertained until the very last second.

Watch
BLOOPERS: How Animals Eat Their Food – MisterEpicMann2

☐ **Video completed**

Date ___/___/___

NOTES:..
....
....

COMEDY INSPIRATION

230. FAILS

One of the earliest types of YouTube comedy video and still going strong – fails never fail to make people laugh.

Prepare
If you don't already have a lot of fail footage you can put together from your own material, you'll have to spend some time trawling through the YouTube archives for funny fail clips.

Film
From cats going crazy to skateboard crashes, pranks backfiring and a whole lot people falling flat on their faces, these videos capture the most epic RL fails that we just can't help but laugh at. You'll need to put your editing skills to work to create your own compilation video of all things fail.

Top Tips
Make sure you ask the person who originally posted the clip for permission to use their clip in your compilation. It's also a good idea to give them credit at the end of the video or in the description box.

Watch
Funny Fails Compilation ||
Best Fails of the year
– FunniestClipsTV

☐ **Video completed**
Date ____/____/____

NOTES:..
....
....

---

231. PRANKS

Whether you like them or loathe them, pranks make up some of the most popular content on YouTube.

Prepare
To pull off the perfect prank, you'll need to spend time planning and setting it up first – you only get one shot to get the perfect reaction. Next, decide who to play your prank on, whether that's a friend, partner or family member – it's best to leave unsuspecting members of the public out of it.

Film
Set up a hidden camera or ask someone else to discreetly film and let the pranking commence! There are lots of different kinds of pranks you could do, from prank calls to spooky set-ups, pranks which incorporate magic tricks or pranks using props such as fake snakes or a disguise.

Top Tips
Always think before you prank. Pranks should always stay firmly on the funny side and never be designed to distress, humiliate or make fun of others.

Watch
Crazy Plastic Ball PRANK!!
– RomanAtwood

☐ **Video completed**
Date ____/____/____

NOTES:..
....
....

COMEDY INSPIRATION

232. FUNNY STORIES

Have a funny story about something that's happened to you IRL? Why not turn it into a video?

Prepare

The best funny stories are based on subjects that people can relate to. Delve into your past to dig up a humorous real life story to tell your viewers. Writing out the main points first will help you to make it as funny as possible – some comedians like to exaggerate their stories a bit for comic effect.

Film

Sit down and tell your story directly to the camera. If you can laugh at yourself, and tell a funny story about it, you'll keep your viewers captivated. Get some mileage out of embarrassing moments or awkward encounters, play up your mistakes and shortcomings, and most of all keep it light in tone.

Top Tips

Pick up some storytelling tips by watching other YouTubers who never fail to make you laugh. This is a great way to figure out the importance of things like comic timing and style.

Watch
Our Awkward Fancy Meal – Daniel Howell

☐ **Video completed**

Date ____/____/____

NOTES:...

....

....

---

233. READING YOUR COMMENTS

The comments section can be a bit of a minefield. What better way to deal with haters than by turning mean comments into a hilarious video?

Prepare

You'll need to wait until you're receiving lots of comments before filming. Compile screenshots of the funniest comments, from lovely ones to the not so nice and the completely nonsensical.

Film

Read out the comments one by one and pass commentary on them. You'll need to have a thick skin to make this kind of video and keep a sense of humour about it all. Put a spin on mean comments by making them funny or irrelevant.

Top Tips

This video is a great way to interact with viewers and connect, so make sure to include a good mix of comments, including some serious comments and questions from viewers too.

Watch
THIS COMMENT IS OFFENSIVE | Reading Your Comments #72 – jacksepticeye

☐ **Video completed**

Date ____/____/____

NOTES:...

....

....

COMEDY INSPIRATION

234. ANIMATION

From short sketches to cartoon series, YouTube is bursting with laugh-out-loud funny animations. If you've got a talent for animating, this is the perfect platform to get your work seen.

Prepare
Try to think of a unique idea for a comedy sketch to animate, whether it's simple and hilariously silly, darkly humorous or outright weird and wacky. Plan it out scene by scene and write your script before getting to work with the animations.

Film
Create a short animation in whatever style you choose. Include a soundtrack to go with your animation once it's complete, including character voices, sound effects and music.

Top Tips
If you're not a pro at animating, that's OK. Plenty of people have made successful channels out of simple drawings and sketch figures, by focusing more on the storytelling and comedy than the quality of the animation. Just look at GradeAUnderA or the asdf series.

Watch
Asdfmovie – TomSka

☐ **Video completed**

Date ___/___/___

NOTES:...
....
....

235. REACTING TO OLD VIDEOS

This classic reaction video is where viewers watch you watching... you. Confused yet? Watch some of your old videos to look back and have a good old laugh at younger you's expense.

Prepare
Wait until you've been on YouTube for a while before making this kind of video – hopefully the quality of your videos will have improved somewhat. This video needs very little preparation, just set up a camera to film your reactions.

Film
Sit back and browse through your YouTube video archives to view some of your very first video uploads. Film your reactions to the screen, as well as overlaying the video you're watching so viewers can laugh (or cringe) along too.

Top Tips
Don't be afraid to show your most embarrassing clips, tear it apart and laugh at your mistakes – that's what makes this video so funny to watch. Let the cringe begin...

Watch
Markiplier Reacting to Old Videos – Markiplier

☐ **Video completed**

Date ___/___/___

NOTES:...
....
....

COMEDY INSPIRATION

236. TAKING ONLINE QUIZZES

Who doesn't enjoy wasting time taking pointless quizzes? We all know them, we all do them, so why not video yourself doing one?

Prepare
Spend some time trawling the Internet to find one or more quizzes to take. You could either base your video around a quiz question theme or just do the dumbest quizzes you can find.

Film
Go on your quiz website of choice and film yourself attempting to take a quiz. They can tell you everything, from whether you're really a mermaid to which YouTuber you'd date, and most importantly, what kind of pizza slice you are.

Top Tips
Don't forget to also record your computer or phone screen as you take the quiz. Insert the footage into the final video in a split screen format.

Watch
YouTube Fangirl Buzzfeed Quizzes (ft. Jim Chapman) | Tyler Oakley – Tyler Oakley

☐ **Video completed**

Date ____/____/____

NOTES:..
....
....

---

237. SPEECH JAMMER CHALLENGE

Do you rarely get tongue-tied? Take on the speech jammer challenge and see if you can still string a sentence together.

Prepare
All you'll need to do is download the speech jammer app (it's free), make sure you have a pair of headphones, and grab a friend.

Film
Take it in turns to ask each other questions while wearing the headphones with the speech jammer app running. The challenge is to try answering like a normal person. The app works by playing your voice back to you at a slower rate while you speak, and makes for a really hilarious video.

Top Tips
You can also film this challenge solo by just trying to talk out loud continuously in front of the camera. Read out part of a book or even try singing a song.

Watch
Speech Jammer Challenge with Mark | Zoella – Zoella

☐ **Video completed**

Date ____/____/____

NOTES:..
....
....

COMEDY INSPIRATION

238. BATTLE OF THE SEXES

These popular videos feature common things that every girl or guy can relate to, often comedically highlighting the differences between the sexes.

Prepare
Come up with a unique idea for your video, playing on the 'what girls and guys do' theme. Explore simple truths and stereotypical differences and turn them into comedy gold.

Film
Act out your sketch in front of the camera and get creative with costumes and props. Examples of this kind of video include 'what girls do on the Internet', 'how guys pack a suitcase' vs. 'how girls pack a suitcase', and 'how girls get ready'.

Top Tips
If you don't already have one, think about investing in a tripod. It's an easy way to keep your camera steady and also perfect for filming your shots hands-free. This means you'll be able to play different character roles yourself.

Watch
How Girls Get Ready...
– IISuperwomanII

☐ **Video completed**

Date ____/____/____

NOTES:...

....

....

239. COMEDY COMMENTARY

This hugely popular style of video combines something everybody loves – viral videos – with hilarious commentaries.

Prepare
Look through YouTube to pick out some of the funniest or most interesting viral videos on the web. You'll basically be reviewing the videos, adding your own witty commentary and jokes, so think about what you want to say and write out some notes or a script.

Film
Either film in front of the camera, presenter-style, or add a voiceover commentary talking about each clip as it happens. Poke fun at the clips, add sound

effects, comment on, parody, or lovingly tear them apart – anything you can to make your video even funnier than the original.

Top Tips
Pick some of the most current viral videos to make sure your video is bang on trend and try to use a catchy title to increase its chances of being found in search.

Watch
SCARIEST RIDE EVER
– Ray William Johnson

☐ **Video completed**

Date ____/____/____

NOTES:...

....

COMEDY INSPIRATION

240. COMEDY ROUTINE VIDEO

Get ready to film a routine-style video with a refreshing twist – it's actually going to be realistic.

Prepare
Plan out how you're going to film your comedy version of a morning routine video, poking a large amount of fun at the typical format.

Film
From pressing snooze on your alarm for the fifteenth time to getting the shampoo in your eyes in the shower, film a funny version of this popular video and make it as realistic or as ridiculous as you like. These videos make a nice change from the unachievable perfection we're usually used to seeing.

Top Tips
It's a good idea to keep a close eye on other YouTube genres to see which videos are trending there. You can put a comedy spin on pretty much anything.

Watch
MY MORNING ROUTINE – Caspar

☐ **Video completed**
Date ____/____/____

NOTES:..
....
....

241. DUBBED/VOICEOVER

Whether it's a hilariously bad dubbing of a popular song or a well-timed voiceover, if you want to go viral, this video is definitely one way to do it.

Prepare
Find a video (or use one of your own) to dub or do a voiceover to. You'll then need to get creative. Write out a script to make sure you include the maximum amount of punch lines and/or randomness (and if it's a clip involving people – to make sure your words match up to their lip movements).

Film
Whether you decide to do a strategically planned voiceover or terribly dubbed singing, give a voice to an inanimate object or something completely unexpected, your audio track has to perfectly match what your viewers are seeing.

Top Tips
The funnier voiceovers out there are when multiple different voices are involved in the dubbing. If you're not the best at voice acting, this kind of video is perfectly suited to getting your friends in on the action.

Watch
"NFL 2015" — A Bad Lip Reading of The NFL – Bad Lip Reading

☐ **Video completed**
Date ____/____/____

NOTES:..
....
....

COMEDY INSPIRATION

242. TRY NOT TO CRINGE

Cringe comedy is a genre of comedy which uses awkward or embarrassing situations to make viewers squirm. Forget the Try Not to Laugh and the Try Not to Cry challenges – the Try Not to Cringe challenge could be the most impossible of them all.

Prepare
Find a ready-made cringe compilation to watch, or scour the depths of YouTube to compile your own list of some of the most cringe-worthy videos in the world.

Film
Set up a camera to film your reactions as you watch the videos. Can you make it all the way through without cringing or laughing? Prepare for facepalming, nervous laughter and feelings of deep discomfort...

Top Tips
Play this challenge game with a friend and award 10 points for each video you can watch in full without cringing. The person with the most points at the end is the king of cringe.

Watch
TRY NOT TO CRINGE CHALLENGE (PewDiePie React) – PewDiePie

☐ **Video completed**

Date ___/___/___

NOTES:..
....
....

---

243. COMEDY SERIES

Who needs TV comedies with all the innovative web shows YouTube has to offer? If you have acting skills or are full of funny ideas for sketches, why not shoot your own comedy series?

Prepare
Brainstorm ideas for your comedy series. Next you'll need to write a script for your first episode – it helps if you've already planned out where you want the series to go. Map out a beginning, middle and an end.

Film
For this one you'll act, direct and do it all. Enlist some mates to help play the other character roles in your series. Be prepared on the day of shooting with the props and costumes that you need and record several readings of the lines so you have enough to work with when it comes to editing.

Top Tips
Get some friends involved in your series. Having other people to help with brainstorming ideas, acting and filming will not only make the process much easier (and more fun) for you, it will also make your video look more professional.

Watch
Oscar's Hotel | KickthePJ – KickThePj

☐ **Video completed**

Date ___/___/___

NOTES:..
....
....

COMEDY INSPIRATION

244. STAND-UP COMEDY

Too scared to do your stand-up comedy routine in front of a live audience? Do a stand-up routine on camera and upload it for (potentially) millions of people to see online instead.

Prepare
Get your best material ready and practice it several times. As well as helping you to memorise the jokes and sound more natural, it'll also help you fine-tune the best way of delivering your punch lines.

Film
Film your routine but whatever you do, make sure your audio is good so everyone's in on the joke.

Watch
Anjelah Johnson - Nail Salon (Stand Up Comedy) – Comedy Time

☐ **Video completed**
Date ___/___/___

245. ANIMALS & BABIES

Animals and babies have been the holy grail for funny YouTube videos since the beginning. You won't even have to be in the video.

Prepare
From funny four-legged animal fails (especially cats) to babies doing adorable things, these hilarious clips can't be planned, so always keep the camera handy. These videos are some of the most likely to go viral.

Film
Babies and animals can often do the funniest things so always keep your camera rolling when you're around them!

Watch
The two talking cats – TheCatsPyjaaaamas

☐ **Video completed**
Date ___/___/___

246. RANDOM

Sometimes, just being a bit weird is the best way to stand out from the rest of the comedy crowd.

Prepare
Think of something original, random or just weird that you can turn into a vid. It might just catch on.

Film
Whether it's eating a picture of a celebrity, replacing audio with the sound of a goat screaming or basing a whole channel around smashing eggs onto stuff, you'll need to film something that no one else has thought to do on YouTube yet.

Watch
I Eat a Picture of Jason Segel Everyday Until He Eats A Picture of Me. Day 1 – Dog Shirt

☐ **Video completed**
Date ___/___/___

COMEDY IDEAS

Write down 10 of your own ideas for comedy videos to film next. Whether it's a prank, a new sketch idea or a hilarious how-to guide, keep your viewers laughing.

247

....
....
....
....

248

....
....
....
....

249

....
....
....
....

250

....
....
....
....

251

....
....
....
....

252

253

254

255

256

NOTES:

COMEDY NOTES

BOOKS & EDUCATION

From BookTube channels, spreading the joys of reading across the web, to education channels dedicated to sharing all kinds of knowledge, YouTube has never been a better place to share something you're passionate about. If you're bonkers about books, fascinated by facts and science or in the know about current news, this is the place for you.

CHANNEL INSPIRATION:

booksandquills: With short, snappy book reviews and recommendations ranging from YA to sci-fi to classic literature, Sanne Vliegenthart is sure to expand your reading horizons.

polandbananasBOOKS: Christine is the biggest BookTuber out there, thanks to her hilarious personality and sheer enthusiasm for the subject. Check her out for hyperactive reviews, relatable book feels, challenges and bookish comedy.

vlogbrothers: Author John Green and brother Hank take turns vlogging about all kinds of topics, from book chat to nerdfighting and explaining complex news. They also run educational channels CrashCourse and SciShow, packed full of geeky goodness.

BOOKS & EDUCATION INSPIRATION

257. BOOK HAUL

BookTube has its own version of the ever-popular haul video, but all about books. Use this opportunity to show off all your latest book buys.

Prepare
Save up all the books you've bought, been given, or borrowed over a period of time, to showcase them all at once in one big book haul. These can range from three books to over 50.

Film
Show each book to the camera one by one and list all the relevant information about it – the book title, the author, whether it's a standalone or part of a series, what it's about (no spoilers) and your first impressions of it.

Top Tips
Be enthusiastic. One of the best things about hauls is to see how excited people are to see and talk about their new books. Your video should encourage your viewers to find books that they can get excited about too!.

Watch
Big May Book Haul!! – PeruseProject

☐ **Video completed**
Date ___/___/___

NOTES:..
....
....

258. BOOK REVIEW

Share your thoughts and honest opinions about a book you've recently read, and help viewers decide whether they'd like to read it too.

Prepare
The best book reviews are well thought out and concise, so it might help to jot down the main points you want to discuss before making your video.

Film
Introduce the book to viewers before giving a brief outline of the plot and sharing your thoughts and feelings about it. Above all, you should be honest and offer your true opinions on the book, be it good or bad. Everybody has a different viewpoint, and other people will find it useful to hear yours.

Top Tips
Book reviews are usually spoiler free, but you should definitely mention beforehand if you are going to give away any major plot points so you don't ruin it for anyone.

Watch
Book Review | Fangirl by Rainbow Rowell. – booksandquills

☐ **Video completed**
Date ___/___/___

NOTES:..
....
....

BOOKS & EDUCATION INSPIRATION

259. BOOKSHELF TOUR

Other YouTubers give house tours and room tours, so it's only natural that BookTubers should give a bookshelf tour. Get ready to give your viewers some serious shelf inspo.

Prepare
Whether it's organised by genre, alphabetically or by the colours of the rainbow, make sure your bookshelf is looking pretty before filming.

Film
Talk viewers through your bookshelves shelf-by-shelf, showing each book individually and naming the title and author. These videos usually have a voiceover, and some also like to showcase their creative editing skills. It can also run a bit longer than other videos since there are often so many books to get through.

Top Tips
Bookshelf tours are a good video introduction into a vlogger's reading tastes and personality, so be sure to show yours off to the max.

Watch
BOOKSHELF TOUR | 2017
– A Clockwork Reader

☐ **Video completed**
Date ___/___/___

NOTES:..
....
....

260. RECOMMENDS

Perfect for anyone looking to find some great new books to read. Make your own video sharing your best book recommendations and viewers will soon be turning to you for all their reading list needs.

Prepare
Whether it's young adult fiction, classic literature or graphic novels, come up with a list of books that you think your viewers need to read right now. Think about what you want to say about each one.

Film
Show each of your recommends to the camera and tell viewers very briefly what the book is about and why you enjoyed it so much. Why not make a seasonal video sharing your top reading picks for the summer holidays or Christmastime too?

Top Tips
Engage your audience by asking for their book recommendations too. If you read any, don't forget to give a shout-out and you can share your thoughts on those books in another video.

Watch
BOOK
RECOMMENDATIONS!
– readbyzoe

☐ **Video completed**
Date ___/___/___

NOTES:..
....
....

BOOKS & EDUCATION INSPIRATION

261. TBR

TBR, or To Be Read videos are super easy to film – just let viewers in on the pile/shelf/room full of books you're yet to crack open. It might motivate you to get on and read them, too.

Prepare
Collect up all of your TBR books to show in your video. These are all of the books that you own, but haven't yet read. You could talk about the books that you want to read but don't own yet too.

Film
Go through your TBR pile one by one. Briefly mention each book and why it's on your to-read list, or why you haven't got round to it yet. Talk about any that you're especially excited to read.

Top Tips
Post this video at the beginning of the month or season as a way to share with viewers which books you plan to read next. They might get some ideas for their own TBR pile.

Watch
ALL OF MY TBR BOOKS!!!!!!! – Bookables

☐ **Video completed**
Date ___/____/____

NOTES: ....
....
....

262. WRAP UP

Make a wrap up video at the end of every month to share your thoughts on all the books you've managed to read that month.

Prepare
Write down a few points about each book after you've finished reading it. Wrap ups are a bit like a shorter book review, so this will help jog your memory when you get round to making the video.

Film
Show each book to your viewers and give a short summary of each. Include your thoughts on the book and talk about whether you enjoyed it or not, and the reasons why.

Top Tips
You don't need to go out and buy a lot of books to be able to make these videos. Many BookTubers have lots of books because they receive free copies from publishing companies for review. You can pick up books for less from charity shops or borrow them from the library.

Watch
February Wrap Up! – Hailey in Bookland

☐ **Video completed**
Date ___/____/____

NOTES: ....
....
....

BOOKS & EDUCATION INSPIRATION

263. BOOKTUBE NEWBIE TAG

Book tags make for some of the most popular BookTube content, and they're also lots of fun to do. This is the perfect tag to introduce yourself to new viewers and fellow YouTubers alike.

Prepare
Compile a list of the BookTube Newbie Tag questions to answer from the Internet and feel free to come up with your own too. Let viewers in on your favourite book genres, why you love to read and what you'll be bringing to BookTube.

Film
Why did you start this channel? What book or series got you into reading? What kind of books do you like to read? These are some of the kinds of questions you can answer when you sit down to film your video.

Top Tips
Since this is an introductory video, make sure you let your personality shine. Be enthusiastic and get viewers excited for the kind of content they can expect to see on your channel in the future.

Watch
Booktube Newbie TAG!
– Reads and Daydreams

☐ **Video completed**
Date ___/___/___

NOTES:...
....

264. READATHON

Have a huge pile of unread books that you want to finally finish? Why not take on a readathon and see how much you can finish in a set amount of time.

Prepare
Readathons usually take place over a set period of time – 24 hours/a week/a month – so choose to do it when you have a lot of spare time to dedicate to reading. Compile your TBR pile of the books you want to read and make sure it's something you're excited about reading.

Film
Find a quiet place to read and vlog your readathon journey. Let viewers know what books you plan to read at the beginning of the vlog and remember to regularly film during the readathon period to give updates on how you're getting on.

Top Tips
Find some friends to take part with you for motivation and to spark your competitive side. There are also events like BookTubeathon, which is a week of reading sprints guided by popular BookTubers, with fun challenges to take part in too.

Watch
24 HOURS OF READING? |
READATHON VLOG
– readbyzoe

☐ **Video completed**
Date ___/___/___

NOTES:...
....
....

BOOKS & EDUCATION INSPIRATION

265. BOOK COMEDY

Whoever said that books were boring? Make a funny bookish comedy sketch or parody video that fellow book worms will instantly relate to.

Prepare
Think of an original way to turn something book-related into a comedy video. You could act something out in a parody or sketch or use humour other readers can relate to, from avoiding book spoilers to the mourning period after a book ends and finding a comfy reading position.

Film
Whether it's a song about overdue library books, a sketch taking book titles literally, a parody of Harry Potter, or relatable comedy about book-related feels, just have fun filming your video.

Top Tips
Promote your video on all of your other social media platforms to maximise the amount of views your video receives and increase the chances of it getting shared around.

Watch
LITERAL BOOK TITLES
– polandbananasBOOKS

☐ **Video completed**
Date ___/___/___

NOTES:...
....
....

266. DISCUSSIONS

Recently read a book that you're just dying to discuss with others? Start your own book-based discussion to share your thoughts with the BookTube community.

Prepare
Decide on a book, theme or question to base your discussion around. For example, you could discuss plot theories about a book you just read, talk about book to movie adaptations or start your own virtual version of the good old-fashioned book club.

Film
Simply get in front of the camera to share your thoughts. Whereas book reviews are usually spoiler-free, discussions are a free for all and you can discuss literally anything and everything you thought about the book.

Top Tips
Some YouTubers even team up and use Google Hangouts to do live book discussions together. Find some friends or fellow BookTubers to debate with, and announce the book you're all going to be reading a month ahead so viewers can join the discussion too.

Watch
FINDING AUDREY
LIVESHOW I
BOOKSPLOSION
– polandbananasBOOKS

☐ **Video completed**
Date ___/___/___

NOTES:...
....

BOOKS & EDUCATION INSPIRATION

267. BOOK SERIES I WON'T FINISH

Too many books too little time? There's no point wasting time finishing a series you don't want to read so why not use that time to make a video about them instead?

Prepare
Go through your bookcase and dig out any books you have that are part of a series that you haven't completed. Be honest with yourself about whether you're going to read the rest or not.

Film
Talk about the series you won't be completing and show the books to the camera if you have them. Give the reasons why you won't be completing the rest, and don't be afraid to voice unpopular opinions

– there's bound to be others who thought the same.

Top Tips
You might hear some YouTubers use the abbreviations DNR or DNF when they didn't like a book and so didn't finish it. These stand for Did Not Read and Did Not Finish.

Watch
SERIES I WON'T FINISH
– Katytastic

☐ **Video completed**

Date ____/____/____

NOTES:..
....
....

---

268. OPINION VIDEO

Do you feel like you have something important to say? Take a stance and make a video about it.

Prepare
If something's got you fired up and you want to share it with the world, do your research first and write down the main points you want to get across.

Film
This video doesn't necessarily have to be about books, it could be an important issue you believe in: politics, feminism or even about the YouTube community itself. Sit or stand in front of the camera and talk passionately about your chosen subject.

Top Tips
Choose to talk about the things you're passionate about – that you really love or really hate – because those feelings and emotions shine through the camera. Even if not everyone shares your views, viewers will respect you for taking a stand.

Watch
Some Rough Advice for the "Real World"
– vlogbrothers

☐ **Video completed**

Date ____/____/____

NOTES:..
....
....

BOOKS & EDUCATION INSPIRATION

269. VIDEO INTERVIEWS

Do you know some interesting people? Do an in-depth interview with them so your viewers can get to know them too.

Prepare
Book vloggers sometimes interview authors to give exclusive reviews, news and cover reveals, but you can choose to interview whoever you like. Friends, family, strangers on the street... the opportunities here are endless. Decide on some questions you want to ask before filming.

Film
Set up a camera to film both you and your interviewee – if you're filming on the street you might want to enlist the help of another person to film for you. Ask them about their daily lives, career, what's going on in the world right now or take a lighter approach and ask random questions.

Top Tips
Make sure you have an external microphone or that the audio is loud enough to hear both the question and the answer, especially if your interview is taking place outside.

Watch
AN INTERVIEW FROM OLYMPUS | Rick Riordan & tiernanbe – TheBookTuber

☐ **Video completed**
Date ____/____/____

NOTES:...
....

270. UNHAULS

Are your shelves cluttered with books you'll never read or pick up again? In a creative twist on the traditional haul concept, for this video you'll actually need to get rid of books rather than buy new ones.

Prepare
Get your TBR pile under control by going through your bookcase and taking out any books you want to sell, donate or give away to friends – you'll show these in your video.

Film
Show your 'unhaul' of books to the camera and go through them one by one. Tell viewers why you've decided to get rid of the book, whether that's because your reading tastes have changed, you have more than one copy or you just aren't interested in reading it.

Top Tips
Don't just throw your books away – even if nobody you know is interested in reading them you can always donate them to a charity shop or local library.

Watch
BOOK UNHAUL #4 – Little Book Owl

☐ **Video completed**
Date ____/____/____

NOTES:...
....
....

BOOKS & EDUCATION INSPIRATION

271. CURRENT EVENTS

Do you frequently find yourself telling friends and family about recent events that have been in the news? Make a video about it and you'll have lots of other people to keep in the loop too.

Prepare
Find a news article that has caught your attention recently, and think about your reactions to it. Do your research before making a video about it to make sure you have the most up-to-date information possible.

Film
Whether you're sharing your own opinion on an event, filling viewers in on existing content (such as a study or an article), or diving into its historical context, your video should be factual, easy to understand and current. If you already have an older video that exists on a similar subject, use annotations to link the older video to the updated one.

Top Tips
If you want to stay ahead of the crowd, frequently check what news topics are trending on Twitter and Facebook and make a video on them.

Watch
Brazil's Government is Falling Apart...and it's Good News? – vlogbrothers

☐ **Video completed**

Date ____/____/____

NOTES: ....
....

272. WORLD BOOK DAY

World Book Day takes place every year to celebrate authors, illustrators, books and (most importantly) reading. If you're a fan of all things books, why not make a video to celebrate?

Prepare
You can pretty much upload any video you like on this day, so long as it's book-related. Brainstorm some fun ideas for bookish videos to make.

Film
Whether you choose to get in on the fancy dress action and dress up as your favourite book character, do a huge haul or talk about your best-loved books and authors, make sure you share and promote the joys of reading with your viewers.

Top Tips
As well as World Book Day, think about unique video ideas you could do to mark other literary holidays, such as National Poetry Month (April) and Shakespeare Day (23rd April).

Watch
Dress up as Greg Heffley | Diary of a Wimpy Kid | Costume idea | World Book Day – Puffin Books

☐ **Video completed**

Date ____/____/____

NOTES: ....
....
....

BOOKS & EDUCATION INSPIRATION

273. BOOK TOWER CHALLENGE

There are plenty of fun book related challenges that spread across YouTube, including bookshelf scavenger hunts like the epic Book Tower Challenge.

Prepare
All you'll need is a bookshelf full of books and the list of 20 challenge questions, which you can find online. Set yourself three minutes to complete the challenge and you're ready to go.

Film
The aim is to answer each question by pulling a book that meets the requirements out of your bookcase and using it to build a tower, e.g. the first book in a series, or a book with blue on the cover. Once you've found them all you then need to do is to arrange them alphabetically within the time to complete the challenge.

Top Tips
If you have enough books, why not compete against friends and up the entertainment factor – the first person to complete their tower wins.

Watch
THE BOOK TOWER CHALLENGE
– polandbananasBOOKS

☐ **Video completed**
Date ___/___/___

NOTES:..
....

274. FESTIVE CHRISTMAS BOOK TAG

With the perfect mix of questions relating to Christmas and to books, this is the ideal book tag to film during the festive season.

Prepare
Find the questions to the festive book tag on YouTube and think through your answers before filming. Look out for any of the books you plan to mention so you can show them during the video.

Film
There are eight Christmas themed bookish questions for you to answer in front of the camera, from the fictional family that you would like to spend Christmas with, to naming a book or character that deserves to be on the 'naughty list'.

Top Tips
Tag another YouTuber to answer the questions too, and don't be afraid to tag people who have more subscribers than you. Tags are a great way to connect and make friends in the YouTube community.

Watch
FESTIVE CHRISTMAS BOOK TAG
– jessethereader

☐ **Video completed**
Date ___/___/___

NOTES:..
....
....

BOOKS & EDUCATION INSPIRATION

275. RESPONSE VIDEO

Making a video response to a popular YouTuber's video can be a great way to continue a discussion, interact with the community and get some extra visitors to your own channel too.

Prepare
Find a popular video related to whichever topic you're interested in and think of some interesting or creative ways you could respond with another video.

Film
Use your video response to start or continue a conversation on YouTube, whether you agree with what they said or disagree. Put the link to the original video you're responding to in the description box and include the creator's name in the video. You may even open up an opportunity to collaborate with them.

Top Tips
Why not make a video response to another BookTuber's review? Linking to it in the comments section of their video adds to the discussion and also draws attention to your own channel, making others more likely to stumble across it and subscribe.

Watch
THE LITERARY CANON | VIDEO RESPONSE – Books Beauty Ameriie

☐ **Video completed**

Date ____/____/____

NOTES: ....
....
....

---

276. GUESS THAT BOOK CHARACTER

Do you know your Dumbledore from your Katniss Everdeen? Play the Guess That Book Character game to really put your novel knowledge to the test.

Prepare
All you'll need for this challenge is some post-it notes and some friends to play the game with. Set your camera up and make sure you're all in the frame before starting.

Film
Each of you should write a book character's name on a post-it note and stick it on another player's forehead. Take it in turns asking questions and guessing which character you are from the hints other players give you. For each correct guess you

get a point and a new name to guess – the person with the most points at the end wins.

Top Tips
BookTube is a very creative community with new tags and challenges popping up all the time. Why not try to come up with one of your own?

Watch
Heads Up: Book Character Edition w/ TheBookTuber – abookutopia

☐ **Video completed**

Date ____/____/____

NOTES: ....
....

BOOKS & EDUCATION INSPIRATION

277. EXPLAIN SCIENTIFIC CONCEPTS

Educate, entertain and blow viewers' minds by tackling scientific subjects and answering some of life's most interesting questions.

Prepare

Choose a scientific concept to explain or a question to answer, such as 'how do magnets work?' Or 'why do we find things creepy?' Do your research and think about how to present the information in an entertaining and easy-to-understand way.

Film

Whether you choose to vlog about an interesting topic, break something down with an animation or conduct a real experiment, explain your scientific concept simply in terms that anyone would be able to understand, and above all, make learning fun.

Top Tips

Whether it's about Science, or Maths or History, sharing what you know on YouTube is a great way to let viewers in on a subject you're passionate about, and teach them something in the process.

Watch
What If Everyone JUMPED At Once? – Vsauce

☐ **Video completed**
Date ____/____/____

NOTES:..
....

278. TOP 5 WEDNESDAY

This weekly book meme started back in 2013 and is still going strong. Get involved by sharing your top 5s of everything to do with books, every Wednesday.

Prepare

Check out the Top 5 Wednesday topics for the coming month online on the Goodreads group or pick a topic of your own to do – there are so many to choose from. Write down your top 5 before filming.

Film

Get in front of the camera to count down your top 5 books related to the particular topic, whether that's your top 5 favourite authors, top 5 character names, top 5 book covers or top 5 characters you want to be your best friend. Don't forget to tell viewers the reasons why each made it on to your list.

Top Tips

Many bookish YouTubers use their bookshelves as a backdrop, so viewers instantly know what their channel and videos are all about. Do a test shot to make sure your background is on point before filming your video.

Watch
Books I Read in One Sitting I Top 5 Wednesday – Thoughts on Tomes

☐ **Video completed**
Date ____/____/____

NOTES:..
....
....

BOOKS & EDUCATION INSPIRATION

279. COLLABORATE

Who says reading has to be antisocial? BookTube may be one of the smaller YouTube communities, but because of that it's one of the easiest places to make friends to collab with.

Prepare
A good way to reach out to other YouTubers is by commenting on a video or tweeting them with a genuine question to get a conversation going before asking them to collaborate.

Film
There are lots of ways to get involved making videos with other BookTubers, from BookTubeathon to book tags, challenges and live discussions. Most importantly, have fun. It's a very welcoming and interactive community and your viewers should feel part of it through watching your videos.

Top Tips
Collabs can play a big part in the success of your YouTube channel. Not only are they a great way to make new friendships, but viewers love watching them and it's a good way to get your videos seen by another person's audience.

Watch
ONE WORD BOOK CHALLENGE | COLLABSPLOSION – Katytastic

☐ **Video completed**
Date ___/___/____

NOTES:..
....

280. BOOK ADAPTATION

You've already heard of book to movie adaptations, but what about making your very own book to YouTube adaptation?

Prepare
Think of a book you love that you could turn into a web series or sketch for YouTube. Get your creative juices flowing and use it to write your own script based around the book, its characters and themes.

Film
Whether you're updating a classic into a modern-day version of events, creating a spin off about what happens next or putting a comedy spin on your favourite passage, enlist some friends to act out your script with, dress up as fictional characters and film the whole thing.

Top Tips
Why not include YouTube and modern technology in your plots? Some adaptations use vlogging into a camera as a device through which to tell modern versions of familiar stories – updating everything from Jane Austen to Shakespeare for the Internet era.

Watch
My Name is Lizzie Bennet - Ep: 1 – The Lizzie Bennet Diaries

☐ **Video completed**
Date ___/___/____

NOTES:..
....
....

BOOKS & EDUCATION INSPIRATION

281. WEIRD FACTS

Are you a fountain of weird and wacky knowledge? Share some strange facts in a video that's sure to blow your viewers' minds.

Prepare
Do your research to find some interesting trivia to share. Think about how you'll present it in a video, whether that's a top 10 list based around a theme, facts which bust myths or just one big jam-packed fact video.

Film
Make an infotainment video sharing any kind of funny, eye-opening, educational, mysterious, little-known or creepy facts from around the world. Make sure you share your trivia in an exciting way – whether you're presenting in front of the camera or using pictures, doodles or animations to illustrate.

Top Tips
These videos are often snappy in nature for fun, straight-to-the-point learning. People have short attention spans so use jump cuts to cut out filler words like 'um', and any awkward pauses.

Watch
50 AMAZING Facts to Blow Your Mind! #1 – MatthewSantoro

☐ **Video completed**
Date ___/___/___

NOTES:...
....
....

282. VIDEO ESSAY

This is your opportunity to release your inner geek and talk about a topic you're passionate about.

Prepare
Like a cross between a documentary and a written essay, video essays explore in-depth ideas on a particular topic. Choose your topic and write a structured essay before filming, including an introduction, your main argument and a conclusion.

Film
Using your essay as a script, record a voiceover for your video, adding images, sounds and video clips afterwards which go with the narration. Whether your topic is to do with books, art, culture, science, politics, films, philosophy or something else, your video will need to be structured, persuasive, and really explain something to your viewers.

Top Tips
Try to take a look at a popular topic from an interesting angle or unique point of view to make your video stand out. Check out some other online essays to see how it's done.

Watch
Harry Potter & The Prisoner of Azkaban: Why It's The Best – Nerdwriter1

☐ **Video completed**
Date ___/___/___

NOTES:...
....
....

BOOKS & EDUCATION IDEAS

Write down 10 interesting ideas for videos based around books and education. Why not keep book fans in the loop on the latest book to movie adaptations, or explain a subject you find fascinating?

283

284

285

286

287

288

289

290

291

292

BOOKS & EDUCATION NOTES

FOOD

Food is one of the fastest growing categories on YouTube, with channels to cater to every taste. As well as cooking tutorials, recipes and tips, you'll find funny food challenges, extreme eats, taste tests and fitness fanatics. Fancy yourself as a master chef? Why not get stuck in?

CHANNEL INSPIRATION:

Niomi Smart: Niomi is always on hand to inspire viewers to eat smarter. Make her your go-to-girl for healthy eating ideas, fitness inspo and general advice on how to look, live and feel better from the inside out.

SORTEDfood: These four friends make cooking fun, sharing their budget-friendly, easy-to-make recipes along with a large helping of banter, challenges and entertaining collabs.

Rosanna Pansino: Rosanna has baked her way to millions of subscribers with her deliciously dorky Nerdy Nummies series. Check it out for tasty themed treats based on video games, TV shows, books and films.

FOOD INSPIRATION

293. COOKING TUTORIAL

More and more people are going to YouTube to get cooking tips, inspiration and guidance. Upload your own tasty tutorials to be the person they turn to.

Prepare

Decide on a dish that you'll teach viewers how to make and get all the ingredients you'll need. It doesn't really matter if you're an amateur or advanced cook, you can teach anything from simple snacks to gourmet dinners.

Film

Guide viewers through how to make the dish step-by-step, using a mixture of wide shots and close-ups showing exactly what you're doing. It's a good idea to show viewers all the ingredients and tools they'll need up front, before getting into the recipe.

Top Tips

It's important to make your cooking tutorials as easy to follow as possible. People enjoy watching cooking videos because they're often easier than reading a recipe – they can copy at their own pace, pausing and rewinding as they go.

Watch

How to make... One Pan Pasta! – Donal Skehan

☐ **Video completed**

Date ___/___/___

NOTES:...
....
....

294. WHAT'S IN MY FRIDGE?

Give curious viewers a little insight into your eating habits by showing them the contents of your fridge.

Prepare

It's a good idea to film this video after you've recently done a food shop, to show viewers the typical items you like to keep in your fridge. There's no point filming if there's nothing in there.

Film

Film a vlog showing the inside of your fridge and going through your food items shelf by shelf. Talk about the kinds of things you'd usually make with the ingredients you have, what your essential food items are and how you usually organise your fridge.

Top Tips

Some foodie YouTubers will show viewers the contents of their freezer too, or even go through the kitchen cupboards.

Watch

WHAT'S IN MY FRIDGE?! – NikkiPhillippi

☐ **Video completed**

Date ___/___/___

NOTES:...
....
....

FOOD INSPIRATION

295. RECIPES

Do you love to come up with your own food creations? Provide viewers with all the foodie inspiration they could need by showing off your own original recipes.

Prepare
Make sure you've practised your recipe to perfection before filming – you don't want to share something that tastes terrible! Get all your ingredients ready within easy reach of where you'll be cooking.

Film
Teach viewers how to try out your recipes from the comfort of their own kitchens. Make it easier for them by listing all the ingredients and measurements they'll need in the description bar as well as during the video.

Top Tips
Upload frequently to build up a back catalogue of recipes to make your channel like a virtual cookbook for viewers to browse through, and you'll have a recipe for success.

Watch
Nutella Popsicle Recipe - Laura Vitale - Laura in the Kitchen Episode 769 – Laura in the Kitchen

☐ **Video completed**

Date ____/____/____

NOTES:...
....
....

296. BAKING

Some of the most popular food channels are entirely dedicated to making delicious deserts. This video will literally be a treat to make.

Prepare
Whether it's cupcakes, cookies, macaroons or crazy-looking cakes, decide on a sweet treat to bake and make sure you have all the ingredients and equipment you need.

Film
Walk viewers through your bake step-by-step, showing what you're doing up close at the same time as you talk through the recipe. Make sure you offer clear instructions on things like oven temperature, cooking time and tools to use.

Top Tips
Baking videos can make a fun upload for all kinds of occasions throughout the year. You could bake something chocolately at Easter, or some spooky themed Halloween treats in October.

Watch
Easter Baking - PASTEL LEMON MERINGUES – AmazingPhil

☐ **Video completed**

Date ____/____/____

NOTES:...
....
....

FOOD INSPIRATION

297. WHAT I EAT IN A DAY

Addictive to watch and fun to film, viewers love to watch What I Eat in a Day food diary videos for some much-need meal inspiration.

Prepare
These videos are like a food-based routine video and can take hours to make since you'll be filming on and off all day. Decide what meals you're going to make and prep your ingredients beforehand to make the cooking part quicker and easier.

Film
Give an insight into your everyday diet by documenting everything you eat in a day, from breakfast through to bedtime. Get out your camera and vlog the process every time you eat, from how you prepare your meals and snacks to the ingredients and measurements used.

Top Tips
You could also film a What I Eat in a Week video, which is where creators share meal plans or shopping lists for everything they eat in a whole week, providing viewers with even more meal ideas.

Watch
18. What I Eat In A Day | Niomi Smart – Niomi Smart

☐ **Video completed**
Date ___/___/___

NOTES: ....
....
....

298. HEALTHY EATING

Health conscious meal ideas are more popular than ever on YouTube. Share your own healthy eating how-tos to help viewers look and feel good from the inside out.

Prepare
From healthy vegan recipes to clean eating ideas, decide on a delicious and nutritious recipe to make that viewers can easily recreate at home.

Film
Whether it's quick and easy lunch ideas or guilt-free desserts, show off your healthy recipes and guide viewers through the cooking process. Film your food creatively – healthy food can often look colourful and pretty so make sure you show it off to its full potential.

Top Tips
Think about the presentation of your food and the close-up shots you want to capture before you start to film. Viewers like to see detailed shots of the food throughout the video, from the raw ingredients to the finished product.

Watch
5 Easy Healthy Breakfast Ideas in Under 5 Minutes – Clean & Delicious

☐ **Video completed**
Date ___/___/___

NOTES: ....
....
....

FOOD INSPIRATION

299. WHAT'S IN MY MOUTH CHALLENGE

Grab a friend and put your taste buds to the test in this hilarious food-based challenge.

Prepare
Before filming, each player will need to pick five food items for the other person to guess. You'll also need a blindfold so there's no peeking and cheating.

Film
Take it in turns to wear the blindfold while the other player puts a food item in your mouth. The challenge is to guess what food it is – the person with the most correct guesses at the end of the game wins.

Top Tips
Some people also play this game with a mixture of food and non-food items. Whatever you do make sure you don't use any items that could be dangerous to taste or swallow.

Watch
"What's in My Mouth" Challenge | Brooklyn and Bailey – Brooklyn and Bailey

☐ **Video completed**

Date ___/___/___

NOTES:..
....
....

---

300. BASIC TECHNIQUES

Help improve your viewers' kitchen abilities by teaching all the basic cooking techniques they need to know.

Prepare
The great thing about this video is you don't need any culinary credentials to make it. Decide on a basic cooking skill to teach to beginners – just make sure you've also mastered it before filming.

Film
Film a tutorial video teaching viewers a standalone skill they can put to use to make delicious dishes at home, from how to chop an onion to poaching the perfect egg. Why not create a whole series of videos, teaching viewers how to cook through YouTube?

Top Tips
Basic skills videos are often highly searched for and can continue to rack up the views long after the upload date. Make sure your titles and thumbnails clearly convey what your video is about, so next time viewers search how to do something they'll stumble across you.

Watch
Poach The Perfect Egg! | Now Cook It – SORTEDfood

☐ **Video completed**

Date ___/___/___

NOTES:..
....

FOOD INSPIRATION

301. EXTREME COOKING

There are lots of food creators on YouTube, so it's important to stand out from the crowd. Some people do this by getting extreme in the kitchen.

Prepare
Brainstorm some creative ideas for a video that's a little bit different from the traditional how-to cooking format. Some channels choose to eat extreme foods or make calorie-bomb concoctions; some do something a little strange, like having a dog narrate their cooking techniques...

Film
Whatever you choose to do, make sure you have fun doing it. Bear in mind that cooking videos don't always have to be educational – many viewers watch them just for sheer entertainment without ever making a thing.

Top Tips
Viewers look for creators with passion, personality and an interesting twist. Find a niche that plays to your particular strengths, whether it's tapping into a trend or putting a comedic slant on teaching skills.

Watch
How to Make Custard Pudding (Recipe) | Cooking with Dog – Cooking with Dog

☐ **Video completed**

Date ___/___/___

NOTES:...
....
....

302. WORLD CUISINES

Have you eaten your way around the world? Why not showcase different types of foods and ways of cooking from all over the globe?

Prepare
Viewers often look to food channels to learn how to cook a new cuisine. Pick an interestingly diverse dish you can teach them.

Film
Whether it's making your own Japanese sushi, Spanish paella or Thai sweet and sour curry, show viewers how to make it step-by-step, including all the things they'll need. You could make your recipe as authentic as possible, or choose to put your own twist on it.

Top Tips
If you're an avid traveller, you could also upload food vlogs and reviews showing viewers the cuisines each of the countries you visit has to offer.

Watch
SUSHI AND SASHIMI: WORLD FOOD – Tonic

☐ **Video completed**

Date ___/___/___

NOTES:...
....
....

FOOD INSPIRATION

303. PIZZA CHALLENGE

You might think eating pizza with a pal sounds like the best video idea ever, but be warned... these pizza toppings come with a twist.

Prepare
You'll need a friend to complete the challenge with you, a normal cheese pizza, as well as 16 mystery pizza toppings hidden in bags. Toppings could be anything from pineapple, olives and pepperoni to chocolate chips, gummy bears, spaghetti and cinnamon.

Film
Take it in turns drawing eight of the mystery pizza toppings each and adding the ingredients to your basic pizzas. Once you've finished, bake the pizza in the oven. You must both eat one entire slice of your crazy topped pizza to complete the challenge.

Top Tips
Food based challenges always go down well on YouTube. Why not come up with one of your own, tag fellow YouTubers to do it and see if it catches on.

Watch
PIZZA CHALLENGE with Chef EvanTubeHD! GROSS Secret Recipe! – EvanTubeHD

☐ **Video completed**

Date ____/____/____

NOTES:...
....
....

304. KITCHEN HACKS

Impress your viewers by teaching them how to pull off cool kitchen tricks that make cooking easier and more fun.

Prepare
Do some research to find the coolest food hacks and kitchen tricks going. From removing strawberry stalks with a straw to cooking eggs in the microwave and cutting watermelon like a boss, the more you can pack into a short, snappy video the better.

Film
Teach viewers how to pull off your cooking hacks. Focus the camera on your hands to show what you're doing at each stage and add a clear voiceover in afterwards for best results.

Top Tips
These videos are extremely popular on YouTube. Make your thumbnail deliciously clickable by adding a clear, close-up picture of one of your cool food hacks to encourage viewers to choose your video above others.

Watch
5 Amazing Food Life Hacks Everyone MUST Know! – CrazyRussianHacker

☐ **Video completed**

Date ____/____/____

NOTES:...
....
....

FOOD INSPIRATION

305. KITCHEN TOUR

Often a very requested video, take your viewers on a grand tour of your kitchen to show them where the food magic happens.

Prepare
Make sure your kitchen is clean and tidy before filming, with everything in its rightful place – viewers don't want to see last night's dirty dishes.

Film
Either film the video vlog-style or ask a friend to film you as take viewers on a 360-degree tour of your kitchen. Show off your prized cooking equipment, share storage solutions and even give a sneaky peek into your cupboards.

Top Tips
Include links to any equipment or decorations that you talk about in the description bar so viewers can easily find it and buy for their own kitchens if they wish.

Watch
KITCHEN TOUR!
– kawaiisweetworld

☐ **Video completed**
Date ___/___/___

NOTES:...
....
....

306. VALENTINE'S DAY TREATS

Spread the love this Valentine's Day with sweet treat tutorials that viewers can make at home for all their loved ones.

Prepare
From heart-shaped cookies to pink-covered cupcakes, decide on a few cute Valentine's Day treats to include in your video and get all the ingredients you need.

Film
Guide viewers through how to make each of your Valentine's Day themed goodies step-by-step. Make sure you upload your tutorial in plenty of time before Valentine's Day and use relevant tags to maximise your views.

Top Tips
There are all kinds of foodie Valentine's Day videos you could choose to make, from healthier treat tutorials to trying Valentine's themed candy.

Watch
Valentine's Day Treats & DIY Gift Ideas! – Bethany Mota

☐ **Video completed**
Date ___/___/___

NOTES:...
....
....

FOOD INSPIRATION

307. VEGAN

Complete this video for November 1st

Veganism is taking the YouTube world by storm, with a whole host of channels helping viewers to live a vegan lifestyle. Why not join in and upload your own vegan recipe in time for World Vegan Day (November 1st).

Top Tips
Many people feel overwhelmed when transitioning to a vegan or vegetarian diet and need new meal ideas and inspiration. If it's something you're passionate about it, make videos to help them out.

Prepare
Brush up on your vegan knowledge and practise making some delicious meat, egg and dairy-free dishes that you can share with viewers.

Film
Whether you're a vegan yourself or just getting in on the veggie trend, film a video sharing some cooking tips, nutritional advice and recipes for vegans. If you are already a vegan, share your top tips and experiences about it too.

Watch
VEGAN RECIPES FOR LAZY DAYS – Liv's Healthy Life

☐ **Video completed**

Date ____/____/____

NOTES:...
....
....

308. TASTE TESTS

Some creators are less about the cooking and all about the eating. Take yourself on a food adventure, sampling snacks and cuisines from around the world for the very first time on camera.

Top Tips
Some YouTubers are sent snacks to try by their subscribers, or you can often find a world foods section in some supermarkets. Unsurprisingly, some of the most popular taste testing videos revolve around tasting candy.

Prepare
Get your hands on some interesting foods. Whether it's chocolate and candy from every culture, cereals, space food or even bugs, you should be open to taste testing anything.

Film
Film your video just as you would a reactions video, trying out foods in front of the camera and offering your opinions and first reactions. These videos are usually light-hearted and silly and sure to leave viewers feeling hungry for more.

Watch
AFRICANS TRY AMERICAN CANDY – Caspar

☐ **Video completed**

Date ____/____/____

NOTES:...
....
....

FOOD INSPIRATION

309. PANCAKE ART CHALLENGE

The Pancake Art Challenge is the perfect video upload to share with viewers on Shrove Tuesday. In other words, Pancake Day!

Prepare
As well as a friend to film with, you'll need pancake mix, some squeezy bottles to put it in and cooking utensils. Think of a few ideas for pictures to create – be as ambitious as you like.

Film
Compete in a pancake cook-off challenge to see who can create the most artistic looking pancakes. Go head to head to draw the same thing at the same time using your pancake mix and film the results from above.

Top Tips
Ask viewers to vote whose pancake art they thought was the best. The best part of this video is that you get to scoff the lot after filming.

Complete this video on Pancake Day

Watch
PANCAKE ART CHALLENGE!! – BFvsGF

☐ **Video completed**
Date ____/____/____

NOTES:..
....
....

310. SCHOOL LUNCH IDEAS

Boost viewers' brainpower at school by showing how to prepare nutritious packed lunches at home. This is an ideal video to upload before back to school season starts.

Prepare
Think up some quick and easy lunch ideas that would be perfect for a school packed lunch. Try to include at least three different ideas in your video, and prep your ingredients before filming.

Film
Whether it's healthy lunch ideas, yummy vegan versions or lunch on a budget, guide viewers through each of your recipe ideas, showing how to make them and the ingredients you used.

Top Tips
With most recipe videos, there will probably be steps that you need to speed up or show a time lapse when you come to editing e.g. when chopping ingredients or baking something in the oven.

Watch
Back To School: Easy and Healthy Lunch Ideas! – Bethany Mota

☐ **Video completed**
Date ____/____/____

NOTES:..
....
....

FOOD INSPIRATION

311. FITNESS

Food and fitness go hand in hand. If you're big into fitness, share your top workout tips, routines and tricks to help keep viewers in shape. Who needs a gym membership?

Prepare
Decide on the type of fitness video you want to make. If you're sharing a workout routine you might want to write down the steps and run through it before filming.

Film
Whether you're sharing your morning workout routine, filming a fitness Q&A, or sharing your sporty hobby, be enthusiastic in front of the camera, encourage viewers to get active too and teach them how.

Top Tips
You don't need fancy equipment or a studio to get started making fitness videos – all you really need is a bit of floor space. Set up a camera on a tripod and you're good to go. Plus, viewers will love that they can easily copy along from the comfort of their home.

Watch
Total Body Pilates Workout I POP PILATES – blogilates

☐ **Video completed**

Date ___/___/___

NOTES:..
....
....

312. DIY SUMMERTIME TREATS

Summertime opens up a whole other world of food possibilities perfect for the hotter weather. Share your DIY summer treat ideas to suit any summer party, sleepover or special occasion.

Prepare
Come up with at least three creative summertime recipes to share with subscribers. Typically, summer foods are cooler, lighter and more refreshing due to the warmer weather.

Film
Share some of your favourite summer recipes and snacks, from frozen popsicles to fruit skewers, no-bake cakes to ice cream sandwiches. Why not get creative with filming and show you and your

friends enjoying your treats outside too to fit with the theme of the video.

Top Tips
Make your food look as yummy as possible and insert close-up shots of your finished treats at the beginning of the video to hook viewers' attention and compel them to watch through to the end.

Watch
DIY SUMMERTIME TREATS! – Rosanna Pansino

☐ **Video completed**

Date ___/___/___

NOTES:..
....

FOOD INSPIRATION

313. EAT THE TREND

Make yours the trendiest food channel around, with recipes covering all the latest must-have food crazes. Viewers will flock to you for food ideas that'll be the envy of Instagram.

Prepare
Keep up-to-date with the current food crazes and test out recipes to make your own homemade versions.

Film
Show subscribers how to recreate food crazes at home with a fun, easy-to-follow cooking tutorial and instructions. There are all kinds of cool concoctions to make, from giant pizza slices to cronuts, unicorn frappuchinos and rainbow bagels – or you could even invent your own.

Top Tips
After uploading, add annotations and cards to your video. These are clickable links that encourage viewers to take an action. Direct them to your other recipes or leave links to your channel page and don't forget to ask them to subscribe.

Watch
DIY Starbucks Unicorn Frappuccino I Eat the Trend – POPSUGARFood

☐ **Video completed**

Date ___/___/___

NOTES:..
....
....

---

314. BABY FOOD CHALLENGE

A little bit gross, but always entertaining, this popular challenge is exactly what it says on the tin (or baby-sized jar)... Try out flavours of baby food and film your reactions!

Prepare
Ask a friend to play the challenge with you and get a variety of different baby food flavours to try. If you can, ask someone else to pick out the flavours for you so it's a complete surprise.

Film
Take it in turns with a friend to try different kinds of baby food while blindfolded. Put your taste buds to the test to see if you can guess the ingredients – you get a point for each correct guess.

Top Tips
If you're not feeling quite so brave you can also film a version where you both just have to eat a spoonful of the stuff without the blindfold – sometimes a challenge in itself.

Watch
Ultimate Baby Food Taste Test – Good Mythical Morning

☐ **Video completed**

Date ___/___/___

NOTES:..
....
....

FOOD INSPIRATION

315. FESTIVE FOOD

Get into the holiday spirit by sharing your tried-and-tested festive food recipes that would be perfect for holiday parties or sharing with pals.

Prepare
Plan out a few creative Christmas-themed goodies and have a trial run if you have never made them before to make sure they look good enough to eat. Lay out your ingredients ready to film to show viewers the things they'll need.

Film
Get in front of the camera to guide viewers through your Christmassy cooking process, offering simple step-by-step instructions as you go. From decorating gingerbread houses to making candy cane cupcakes, you'll have lots of fun with the festive theme.

Complete this video as part of Vlogmas

Top Tips
Successful food creators organise their recipes by meal type, occasion, diet or season to make it easy for viewers to find exactly what they're looking for.

Watch
Easy DIY Holiday Party Snacks & Christmas Treats! – LaurDIY

☐ **Video completed**

Date ____/____/____

NOTES: ....
....
....

316. POP CULTURE COOKING

Offer viewers a fun mixture of popular culture and cooking how-tos and you'll soon find you could be racking up the views.

Prepare
Write down a list of characters or objects from your favourite films, books, TV shows, computer games or cartoons. Now write another list full of foods that you like to make. Use these lists to mix and match ideas together to come up with something great.

Film
Whether it's Hello Kitty cupcakes or Harry Potter potion-inspired drinks, whip up your pop culture themed goodies in front of the camera, sharing tips on how to recreate them at home.

Top Tips
Stay on top of global trends, holidays and tent-pole events that viewers are buzzing about, such as big movie releases or new TV shows. Relate your recipes to these and they're sure to generate a lot more interest.

Watch
How to Make PAWPSICLES from Zootopia! Feast of Fiction S5 Ep15 – Feast Of Fiction

☐ **Video completed**

Date ____/____/____

NOTES: ....
....
....

FOOD INSPIRATION

317. TESTING BUZZFEED RECIPES

If you've ever been on social media, you're sure to have been distracted by a tasty-looking BuzzFeed recipe video or two. But are they actually any good? Put some to the test to find out.

Prepare
Find a few recipes on BuzzFeed to try and recreate yourself, and get any ingredients you need.

Film
Get cooking on camera. Once finished, do a taste test and let viewers know what you think, whether there's anything about the recipe you would improve, and give it a score out of 10.

Watch
Microwave Desserts Review!- Buzzfeed Test #3 – David Seymour

☐ **Video completed**
Date ___/___/___

318. GIANT CANDY

These videos are some of the most likely to go viral and it's not hard to see why – who doesn't want giant sized versions of their favourite confectionary?

Prepare
From working out ingredient amounts to finding equipment big enough to make your supersized treat, this one will definitely require some planning out beforehand.

Film
Put your baking skills to the test and film the process from start to finish. Offer step-by-step instructions as you go or add a voiceover.

Watch
GIANT TWIX Candy Bar Recipe – How To Cook That

☐ **Video completed**
Date ___/___/___

319. KITCHEN HAUL

Whether you're redecorating or just having a kitchen supply splurge, share the hauls with your foodie fans.

Prepare
Before you start filming, gather up all of your new kitchen items ready to show in the video.

Film
Film the video in your kitchen setting and show each of your haul items to the camera. Talk about why you got each item, what it's for and/or the delicious things you're planning to make with them.

Watch
KITCHEN HAUL! – Rosanna Pansino

☐ **Video completed**
Date ___/___/___

FOOD IDEAS

Come up with 10 of your own ideas for food-themed videos to film. You could film a cooking collab with a friend, carry out an eating challenge or teach your viewers how to make a treasured family recipe.

320 ....

321 ....

322 ....

323 ....

324 ....

325

326

327

328

329

NOTES:

164

FOOD NOTES

MUSIC

With music videos from every genre, hilarious parodies, original songs and cool covers, YouTube is now the place that most people turn to for music on-demand. It's also the place where bands and artists go to get their music discovered. If you're a talented musician in the making, start uploading your videos now – your future fans are waiting.

CHANNEL INSPIRATION:

Doddleoddle: With a channel packed full of quirky, original songs, ukulele playing, candid vlogs and all-round adorableness, British singer-songwriter Dodie is definitely one to watch.

Troye Sivan: From posting funny vlogs and covers from his room to having chart-topping albums and worldwide tours, Troye has successfully made the transition from YouTuber to fully-fledged musician.

PTXofficial: This powerhouse group create awesome a cappella arrangements of popular songs. Check them out for unique covers, slick music videos and behind-the-scenes vlogs.

MUSIC INSPIRATION

330. SONG COVER

Creating covers of popular songs can be one of the very best ways to get your talent seen on YouTube. Covers allow you to attract the audiences of bigger artist's who might not have found you otherwise.

Prepare
Keep in touch with which songs are currently trending, and try to get your own cover version of the song up on the site as soon as possible.

Film
Film a cover version in front of the camera, making sure the audio is crystal clear – live or pre-recorded it's up to you. It's a good idea to put your own spin on a song and interpret it in your own unique style. Put as much info as you can in your descriptions and tags to aid discovery. If it worked for Justin Bieber...

Top Tips
Include the original artist's name and song title in your own video title and make sure you also include the word 'cover' in the title of the video so viewers don't feel misled and give it a thumbs down.

Watch
"Breakeven" - The Script (ft. Max Schneider) – Kurt Hugo Schneider

☐ **Video completed**
Date ____/____/____

NOTES:..
....
....

331. ACOUSTIC

Do you have some musical talent to share with the world? Whether you have the voice of an angel or are skilled at playing some instrument, perform a song acoustically to really show it off.

Prepare
Pick a popular song to cover acoustically and come up with your own version of it, preferably in your usual music style or genre. Practice several times before you press record.

Film
Whether you're performing an original song or a cover, a chart song or a classic, strip it back and perform your version with no backing track – just you.

Top Tips
Make sure you release new content regularly. Create a video release schedule so that viewers know when your videos are going up and can look forward to it.

Watch
Sweet Creature – Harry Styles (Hannah Trigwell acoustic cover) – Hannah Trigwell

☐ **Video completed**
Date ____/____/____

NOTES:..
....
....

MUSIC INSPIRATION

332. ORIGINAL SONG

As well as covers, instruments and parodies galore, the music community is full of talented singer-songwriters uploading their stuff. If you have an original song to share, this is the platform to pick up exposure.

Prepare
You'll need to have written an original song to perform before doing anything else. If not, brainstorm some ideas for a theme and jot down some lyrics. There are no rules here – you can do anything you like that's not already been done.

Film
Whether it's happy or sad, funny or dramatic, perform your original song in front of the camera in whatever style suits you. Use the end screen and annotations to encourage viewers to leave

comments, likes and shares.

Top Tips
It's really important to promote yourself and your music to other people by using all the social media platforms you can. The more fans can see and share your content with their friends, the more exposure you'll get.

Watch
My Face - original song ||
dodie – doddleoddle

☐ **Video completed**

Date ____/____/____

NOTES:...
....
....

333. MUSIC VIDEO

Music videos are a great way to introduce your music to new fans. Create your own video for one of your standout tracks.

Prepare
Even if you're on a no-budget budget you can still make an entertaining music video. Brainstorm some ideas for a concept that will go with your song and fit the tone. Story board each scene, but allow for spontaneous things to happen during the shoot too.

Film
One of the easiest options is to shoot a traditional music video, filmed with actors in an interesting location. Get your friends involved – you'll most likely need some help directing and shooting the video, and they can act as extras in your video too.

Top Tips
Keep in mind when editing your video together that every frame has to be interesting and flow with the music. Try to match the action to the music and tempo.

Watch
OK Go - Here It Goes
Again – OKGoVEVO

☐ **Video completed**

Date ____/____/____

NOTES:...
....
....

MUSIC INSPIRATION

334. PARODY SONG

Parody songs can make for some of the most popular content on YouTube.

Prepare
Parody songs can take many different forms so decide on what kind of video you want to film and write out some lyrics. Comedy songs often have higher production values, so think about using costumes and props to improve the look of your video.

Film
Whether you're copying a popular song and adding an amusing twist, making a parody of your own music or singing a song so badly it's kind of good, have fun with your video. With funny original lyrics and crazy dance moves, parodies make viewers want to sing – and laugh – along.

Top Tips
Why not create an alter-ego character to perform your song? Coleen Balinger, managed to make a whole channel (and career) out of parody musical character, Miranda Sings.

Watch
LA LA LAND by Miranda Sings – Miranda Sings

☐ **Video completed**
Date ___/____/____

NOTES:..
....
....

---

335. CURRENT FAVOURITE SONGS

Use this video to let viewers in on your musical tastes and give a shout-out to all the songs you're currently loving.

Prepare
What's on your playlist at the moment? Over the course of a week or month, make a list of the songs or albums that you just can't stop listening to.

Film
Sit down in front of the camera to make a chatty video, sharing your favourite songs with subscribers. For each song, play a short clip of it and tell us what it's called, which artist it's by, and when you usually like to listen to it.

Top Tips
At the end of the video, ask viewers what songs they're loving at the moment and to leave a comment with their suggestions for you.

Watch
My Current Favorite Songs/ Playlist – Milica Begecki

☐ **Video completed**
Date ___/____/____

NOTES:..
....
....

MUSIC INSPIRATION

336. TOUR DIARY

Ok, so you might not be touring sell-out stadiums just yet, but this diary-style vlog could include any small gig, playing at a friend's party or even busking.

Prepare
If you're going to be too busy performing to vlog much, think about asking a friend to come along and film for you. It's good to get a mix of the action as well as your vlogged behind-the-scenes insights.

Film
Make a mini documentary style vlog all about your gig experience, from backstage shenanigans to crowd reactions, where you're playing, the people around you, including your personal thoughts on all of it.

Top Tips
Uploading vlogs like these to your channel gives viewers a glimpse into you as a serious musician as well as the personal connection that's gained through a vlog.

Watch
Ed Sheeran: US Tour Diary 2013 (Part 1) – Ed Sheeran

☐ **Video completed**

Date ____/____/____

NOTES:..
....
....

337. THE MUSIC TAG

Whether you're a musician, or simply someone who enjoys music, this tag is designed to give some in-depth insight on your musical preferences.

Prepare
Find the full list of questions for the music tag online and pick and choose from them to create your own list of questions you want to answer.

Film
What's your favourite movie soundtrack? What was the last song you listened to? Which song would you do karaoke to? Most embarrassing song on your playlist? Answer some of these questions when you sit down in front of the camera to talk all about music.

Top Tips
Think about adding subtitles to your videos. Typing out the transcript can be a time consuming task, but according to YouTube it can help to increase your audience.

Watch
Music Tag | lindseyrem – lindseyrem

☐ **Video completed**

Date ____/____/____

NOTES:..
....
....

MUSIC INSPIRATION

338. 'MAKING OF' VIDEOS

'Making of' videos are a great upload idea when you just don't have the time to make fresh content.

Prepare

Next time you're making a music video or a parody production, make sure you capture some extra footage to use for a 'making of' video.

Film

Take viewers behind the scenes of your video shoot in a behind-the-scenes vlog, letting them in on industry secrets, any issues you had and how the whole thing came together.

Top Tips

Alternatively, keep all of the funny outtakes from your video shoot and edit it together to make it into one big bloopers reel.

Watch

Pentatonix - Gangnam Style Bloopers!! – PTXVlogs

☐ **Video completed**

Date ____/____/____

NOTES:..
....
....

339. WOW FACTOR

From the totally bonkers to the insanely impressive, adding a certain 'wow' factor to your music uploads means they're much more likely to go viral.

Prepare

Brainstorm some ideas for music videos you could make that are slightly out of the norm. Look to other off-the-wall music channels for inspiration.

Film

Whether you're using an unusual instrument to make music, singing in a silly voice, making a weird musical mash-up or incorporating some crazy dance moves, the more absurd your videos are, the more they'll be shared.

Top Tips

Why not make music using items you have around the house? Uber successful YouTuber, Andrew Huang, has created hundreds of songs using unusual 'instruments' like balloons, fidget spinners and jeans.

Watch

99 Red Balloons - played with red balloons – ANDREW HUANG

☐ **Video completed**

Date ____/____/____

NOTES:..
....
....

MUSIC INSPIRATION

340. THE DISNEY CHALLENGE

Disney movies are home to some of the catchiest songs of all time... but how well do you really know them? Put your knowledge to test in this fun challenge.

Prepare
You'll need a friend to play the game with and a series of Disney songs to listen to – you can easily find a playlist on YouTube.

Film
Take turns to play Disney songs for the other player to guess. You have 10 seconds to guess both the song title and the film it's from, after which the other person gets to make a guess and steal your points. The person with the most points at the

end is the biggest Disney fan.

Top Tips
Though it's perfectly possible to film with just two people, this challenge will be a lot easier if you ask a third person to choose the song clips in a random order and count down the time each round.

Watch
The Disney Challenge (ft. Zoella) | Tyler Oakley – Tyler Oakley

☐ **Video completed**

Date ___/___/___

NOTES:...

....

---

341. SONGWRITING TIPS

If you've already got a few original songs under your belt, why not share your top songwriting tips to help out other aspiring musicians?

Prepare
Before filming, write out a list of your songwriting advice. Try to aim for around 10 points, from how to think of a topic, to song structure and lyric writing tips.

Film
Sit down in front of the camera to film your video, vlog-style. Talk through your tips one by one, relating them to your own songwriting experiences.

Top Tips
There are lots of other videos you can film to do with songwriting, such as explaining the meanings behind some of your songs, sharing where you get your inspiration from, or asking viewers for feedback on works in progress.

Watch
10 Songwriting Tips for Beginners – EmmaMcGann

☐ **Video completed**

Date ___/___/___

NOTES:...

....

....

MUSIC INSPIRATION

342. LIP-SYNCING

Believe it or not, several big name YouTubers got their start simply by lip-syncing along to popular songs. Show off your miming skills by making one of your own.

Prepare
Lip-syncing is when you attempt to silently match your lip movements to pre-recorded speaking or singing. Pick a song to lip-sync to and practice until you can perfectly nail it.

Film
Get in front of the camera and lip sync to a song to your heart's content. From matching dance moves to goofing around with exaggerated facial expressions – the more effort you put in the better.

Top Tips
You could incorporate compilations from super addictive and popular lip-sync apps like musical.ly as a way to make quick and funny videos.

Watch
YouTube vs. Musical.ly Lip Sync Battle – Rebecca Zamolo

☐ **Video completed**

Date ____/____/____

NOTES:..
....
....

---

343. MUSIC TUTORIAL

If you can play an instrument really well, this video offers the opportunity to show off your skills and teach others at the same time.

Prepare
Decide what kind of music tutorials you want to make. You could show beginners how to play an instrument from scratch, teach music theory, or show people how to play a popular song.

Film
Whether you play the guitar, piano, ukulele or whatever, set your camera up to focus in on your hands as you play so viewers can see what you're doing. Make sure you offer easy-to-follow instructions and high quality audio.

Top Tips
Viewers love online music lessons because they're free and convenient – you can learn at your own speed and pause or rewind when you need. Ask viewers what tutorials they'd like to see you film next.

Watch
How to Play "Let It Go" (Disney's Frozen) Piano Tutorial – PianoKeyz

☐ **Video completed**

Date ____/____/____

NOTES:..
....
....

MUSIC INSPIRATION

344. MUSIC COLLAB

One of the best ways to attract a new audience is to collaborate with other YouTube musicians and creators.

Prepare
Reach out to another creator who has similar subscriber numbers to you so you can grow your channels together, and suggest an idea for a video or work on one together.

Film
Whether you sing a duet or each do your own thing, work in harmony to make each other sound as good as you can – it's not about having a competition. Don't forget to cross-promote each other – think about filming a different video for each of your channels.

Top Tips
Consider collaborations with non-music channels too, to bring a whole new aspect to your music video. You could invite a fashion guru to style your music video or team up with a dance channel to add some cool choreography.

Watch
An Awkward Duet - feat. Jon Cozart ‖ dodie – doddleoddle

☐ **Video completed**
Date ___/____/____

NOTES:...
....
....

345. INTERVIEWS

Give viewers some insider insight by interviewing other musicians, your bandmates, other bands, music industry peeps, your fans, family – even yourself.

Prepare
Find an interesting person to interview and think of a few insightful questions to ask before you start filming. Or, reach out to your subscribers on social media and ask if they have any questions they want answered.

Film
Set up your camera to film you and whoever else you're interviewing, or enlist the help of a cameraman. Ask your list of prepared questions but don't be afraid to just go with the flow and engage with the other persons answers naturally.

Top Tips
If you want to add some music that isn't yours to the background of your video, the YouTube audio library is a great place to get free, no copyright music.

Watch
The Working Musician Interview Series - Sulene van der Walt – JPBouvet

☐ **Video completed**
Date ___/____/____

NOTES:...
....
....

MUSIC INSPIRATION

346. THANK YOU VIDEO

Once you've started to become more established, make a very personal video to thank your subscribers when you reach important milestones in your career.

Prepare
If something great happens to you, share it with your fans. Think through what you want to say before you film your video, and make notes if it will help.

Film
Maybe you've reached a significant YouTube milestone, achieved a musical ambition or even released your first album – whatever the achievement, make a video talking to camera to genuinely thank the people who helped you get there.

Top Tips
Often, YouTubers will also leave a comment underneath their own video that further backs up the sentiment of the video and allows viewers to reply and engage. Always try to reply to a few comments on every video you upload to build a connection with your subscribers.

Watch
The Whole Story
– Troye Sivan

☐ **Video completed**
Date ___/___/___

NOTES:..
....
....

---

347. MUSICAL FIRSTS

Dig deep and share your musical past with viewers to help them get to know you a little better.

Prepare
Jog your memory and jot down some of your musical firsts before filming. This will help you speak more fluently when the camera's rolling.

Film
From the first song you remember listening to, to the first album you ever bought, the first concert you went to and the first song you slow danced to, give viewers the low down on your musical firsts and tell the stories behind them.

Top Tips
You could also make a Musical Firsts video about your own music making past, sharing everything from the first song you wrote to the first music video you made, to show viewers how you got to where you are now.

Watch
MUSICAL FIRSTS
– Weirdly Musical

☐ **Video completed**
Date ___/___/___

NOTES:..
....
....

MUSIC INSPIRATION

348. TRY NOT TO SING ALONG CHALLENGE

This hilarious challenge is surprisingly hard... will you be able to resist singing along to some of the greatest music hits ever?

Prepare
Create your own playlist of catchy songs that you usually can't resist having a sing-along to, or use one of the already curated playlists for this challenge on YouTube.

Film
Sounds easy enough, right? Simply set up a camera to film yourself as you watch the music videos and try not to sing along to the songs...

Top Tips
You can also play a version of this challenge with a friend for even more hilarity. See who cracks and starts to sing first.

Watch
ADULTS REACT TO TRY NOT TO SING ALONG CHALLENGE – FBE

☐ **Video completed**

Date ___/___/____

NOTES:...
....
....

349. BEHIND THE SCENES

Fans love to see what musicians get up to behind the scenes – at music rehearsals, video shoots, recording sessions, on the road or just hanging out – so why not show them.

Prepare
The great thing about this video is it doesn't require much prep at all – just make sure you always have your smart phone or camera on you in case you want to film something.

Film
This should be a casual, vlog style video where you give viewers a glimpse into your world that they usually wouldn't get to see and make content based around what you're already doing.

Top Tips
This is a great video to let viewers get to know you better, connect with your personality and also a way to casually promote your upcoming shows and music.

Watch
Shawn Mendes - "Stitches" Official Video [Behind The Scenes] – Shawn Mendes

☐ **Video completed**

Date ___/___/____

NOTES:...
....
....

MUSIC INSPIRATION

350. BEATBOX

Beatboxing is a rising musical genre on YouTube, where creators produce all kinds of percussion-like sounds just with their mouths. If you have a talent for beatboxing or SFX sounds, upload a video to amaze your viewers.

Prepare
Practice makes perfect. Once you've decided on something to perform, practise it over and over until your beats are on point.

Film
You could show off your sounds solo, have a beatbox battle with someone else, or edit an original song together made entirely from clips of your own beatboxing sounds.

Top Tips
Have more than one skill? Why not combine them to add a twist to your videos that will give you a unique edge. For example, YouTube music megastar Lindsay Stirling became successful by combining her talent for violin with dancing at the same time.

Watch
Beatboxing flute inspector gadget remix – PROJECT Trio

☐ **Video completed**
Date ___/___/___

NOTES: ....
....
....

351. ANNOUNCEMENTS

Actively engage with your audience by sharing the exciting things you've got coming up before they happen.

Prepare
Wait until you have something important you want to share with viewers. Engage on social media to let viewers know you have a video coming before you upload it to create a sense of excitement around your announcement.

Film
Make a vlog announcement any time you want to share special news, such as an upcoming event or tour, a song getting played on the radio, an album release or personal milestone. Make sure you give viewers key information such as dates and places.

Top Tips
Since this is a quick and easy video to make, it's also a good upload to check in with subscribers during busy times when you'd usually be off the radar.

Watch
Announcing My Album. – Troye Sivan

☐ **Video completed**
Date ___/___/___

NOTES: ....
....
....

MUSIC INSPIRATION

352. THE HUMMING CHALLENGE

This fun music challenge puts both your song knowledge and humming skills to the test.

Prepare
Ask a friend to play the humming challenge with you. You should each choose five popular songs to hum before you start filming.

Film
Get in front of the camera and take it in turns to hum a song while the other person tries to guess what it is. You get one point for correctly guessing the name of the song and another for naming the artist – the person with the most points wins (or it just means the other person is really bad at humming).

Top Tips
Make your video as fun to watch as possible. A good tip for editing is to watch the video back in full first. If you find yourself getting bored at any point – those are the parts you should cut out.

Watch
The Humming Challenge (ft. Betty Who) | Tyler Oakley – Tyler Oakley

☐ Video completed

Date ___/___/___

NOTES:..
....
....

353. LYRIC VIDEO

Don't have time to make a full-blown music video for one of your songs? Think about making a lyrics video for it instead. Viewers love to learn the words to a song and sing along!

Prepare
Simple to make but super effective, lyric videos can be a key part of your music channel. Choose one of your songs to turn into a lyric video and think about how to present it in an interesting way.

Film
Your video should display the written lyrics to the song on screen as the music plays, which you should easily be able to do with editing software. Think about the colour scheme, backgrounds and fonts and tailor it to the mood of your song.

Top Tips
Try to create lyric videos that are creative and unique to inspire fans to share your music videos with others.

Watch
Katy Perry - Roar (Lyric Video) – KatyPerryVEVO

☐ Video completed

Date ___/___/___

NOTES:..
....
....

MUSIC INSPIRATION

354. FAN-MADE MUSIC VIDEO

If you don't make music yourself, this video can offer a creative outlet to express yourself. Fan-made videos based on popular hits can become YouTube sensations in their own right.

Prepare
Make your own music video for a song you love. Decide on a creative theme for your video, such as using animation, your own visual story, a picture slideshow or creating a mash-up with another song.

Film
However you decide to make your fan video, try to come up with new and creative ways to get your video seen and shared. Sometimes these videos can be even better than the official versions.

Top Tips
Bear in mind that these videos are in a bit of a grey area when it comes to copyright. Sometimes they can be taken down, but in some cases they receive the support of the artist with monetized ads. If you're an aspiring filmmaker it can prove a great way to get your work seen.

Watch
SAIL - AWOLNATION
(Unofficial Video)
– Nanalew

☐ **Video completed**
Date ____/____/____

NOTES:..

....

355. SHOUT-OUT VIDEO

Spread the love on YouTube with a shout-out video telling the world about the music creators you admire. Who knows, they might even return the favour.

Prepare
Choose a few music channels to talk about – think four or five of your favourites. Think through what you want to say about each of the creators and their channels.

Film
Film in front of the camera to let viewers know which musical YouTubers you regularly watch, what they do on their channel and why you like watching them. This is basically a super supportive video saying nice things about other people and their content.

Top Tips
Include clickable links and information to all the channels you talk about and verbally direct viewers to go and check them out and subscribe too.

Watch
Music Based Channels You
Should Check Out!
– The Music Lab

☐ **Video completed**
Date ____/____/____

NOTES:..

....

....

MUSIC IDEAS

Add 10 of your own original ideas for music videos, from behind-the-scenes activities to instrument set-ups, catering them to your own unique talents.

356

357

358

359

360

361

362

363

364

365

NOTES:

MUSIC NOTES

PLANNING

VIDEO TITLE: **DATE:** _____/_____/_____

GREETINGS AND INTRODUCTION:

MAIN CONTENT:

Use these pages to plan your videos. For in-depth videos where you want to stay on topic it's a good idea to plan out what you want to say. You don't have to script the whole thing, but you could make notes of the key points you want to cover in your video.

KEY POINTS:

SIGN OFF:

NOTES:

PLANNING

VIDEO TITLE:

GREETINGS AND INTRODUCTION:

MAIN CONTENT:

KEY POINTS:

SIGN OFF:

NOTES:

PLANNING

VIDEO TITLE: **DATE:** _____/_____/_____

GREETINGS AND INTRODUCTION:

MAIN CONTENT:

KEY POINTS: ....

....

....

....

SIGN OFF:

NOTES: ....

....

....

PLANNING

VIDEO TITLE: **DATE:** ___/___/___

GREETINGS AND INTRODUCTION:

MAIN CONTENT:

KEY POINTS:

SIGN OFF:

NOTES:

PLANNING

VIDEO TITLE: **DATE:** ____/____/____

GREETINGS AND INTRODUCTION:

MAIN CONTENT:

KEY POINTS:

SIGN OFF:

NOTES:

PLANNING

VIDEO TITLE: **DATE:** _____/_____/_____

GREETINGS AND INTRODUCTION:

MAIN CONTENT:

KEY POINTS: ....

....

....

....

SIGN OFF:

NOTES: ....

....

....

PLANNING

VIDEO TITLE: **DATE:** _____ / _____ / _____

GREETINGS AND INTRODUCTION:

MAIN CONTENT:

KEY POINTS:

SIGN OFF:

NOTES:

PLANNING

VIDEO TITLE: **DATE:** _____/_____/_____

GREETINGS AND INTRODUCTION:

MAIN CONTENT:

KEY POINTS:

SIGN OFF:

NOTES:

PLANNING

VIDEO TITLE: **DATE:** _____/_____/_____

GREETINGS AND INTRODUCTION:

MAIN CONTENT:

KEY POINTS: ....

....

....

SIGN OFF:

NOTES: ....

....

....

PLANNING

1

VIDEO TITLE: **DATE:** _____/_____/_____

GREETINGS AND INTRODUCTION:

MAIN CONTENT:

KEY POINTS:

SIGN OFF:

NOTES:

ANALYTICS

VIDEO TITLE	VIDEO DURATION	DATE UPLOADED	VIEW COUNT	WATCH TIME

Use these pages to record the analytics of your videos. We suggest adding this data in a week after each video went live. Be aware when reviewing your stats that YouTube measures age in ranges, location by country only and gender as binary.

SHARES	REVENUE	MOST WATCHED AGE RANGE	GENDER SPLIT	LOCATION	PLATFORM

ANALYTICS

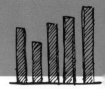

VIDEO TITLE	VIDEO DURATION	DATE UPLOADED	VIEW COUNT	WATCH TIME

SHARES	REVENUE	MOST WATCHED AGE RANGE	GENDER SPLIT	LOCATION	PLATFORM

ANALYTICS

VIDEO TITLE	VIDEO DURATION	DATE UPLOADED	VIEW COUNT	WATCH TIME

SHARES	REVENUE	MOST WATCHED AGE RANGE	GENDER SPLIT	LOCATION	PLATFORM

ANALYTICS

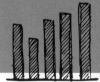

VIDEO TITLE	VIDEO DURATION	DATE UPLOADED	VIEW COUNT	WATCH TIME

SHARES	REVENUE	MOST WATCHED AGE RANGE	GENDER SPLIT	LOCATION	PLATFORM

ANALYTICS

VIDEO TITLE	VIDEO DURATION	DATE UPLOADED	VIEW COUNT	WATCH TIME

SHARES	REVENUE	MOST WATCHED AGE RANGE	GENDER SPLIT	LOCATION	PLATFORM

ANALYTICS

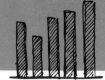

VIDEO TITLE	VIDEO DURATION	DATE UPLOADED	VIEW COUNT	WATCH TIME

SHARES	REVENUE	MOST WATCHED AGE RANGE	GENDER SPLIT	LOCATION	PLATFORM

ANALYTICS

VIDEO TITLE	VIDEO DURATION	DATE UPLOADED	VIEW COUNT	WATCH TIME

SHARES	REVENUE	MOST WATCHED AGE RANGE	GENDER SPLIT	LOCATION	PLATFORM

ANALYTICS

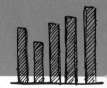

VIDEO TITLE	VIDEO DURATION	DATE UPLOADED	VIEW COUNT	WATCH TIME

SHARES	REVENUE	MOST WATCHED AGE RANGE	GENDER SPLIT	LOCATION	PLATFORM

ANALYTICS

VIDEO TITLE	VIDEO DURATION	DATE UPLOADED	VIEW COUNT	WATCH TIME

SHARES	REVENUE	MOST WATCHED AGE RANGE	GENDER SPLIT	LOCATION	PLATFORM

CREDITS AND ACKNOWLEDGEMENTS

Instagram
58CL © alexwassabi/Instagram; 130TR © booksandquills/Instagram; 112CL © danisnotonfire/Instagram; 166TR © doddleoddle/Instagram; 94BR © funforlouis/Instagram; 94CL © heynadine/Instagram; 112 BR © iisuperwomanii/Instagram; 22CL © jacksepticeye/Instagram; 130 BR © johngreenwritesbooks/Instagram; 76BR © laurdiy/Instagram; 76TR © megandeangelis/Instagram; 40BR © nikkietutorials/Instagram; 148TR © niomismart/Instagram; 58TR © oliwhitetv/Instagram; 22TR © pewdiepie/Instagram; 58BR © pointlessblog/Instagram; 166BR © ptxofficial/Instagram; 148BR © rosannapansino/Instagram; 40CL © samanthamariaofficial/Instagram; 76CL © sarahlynntea/Instagram; 112TR © smosh/Instagram; 148CL © sortedfood/Instagram; 4CL © stardak/Instagram; 40TR © tanyaburr/Instagram; 4BR © theannaedit/Instagram; 22BR © tiffyquake/Instagram; 166CL © troyesivan/Instagram; 94TR © vagabrothers/Instagram; 130CL © xtinemay/Instagram; 4TR © zoella/Instagram.

YouTube
132TR © A Clockwork Reader/YouTube; 140BR © abookutopia/YouTube; 107BR © Alex Chacon/YouTube; 8TR © AlishaMarie/YouTube; 17BR © Amanda Steele/YouTube; 45BR © Amanda Steele/YouTube; 64TR, 150BR © AmazingPhil/YouTube; 89CR © Amy Poehler's Smart Girls/YouTube; 88BR © Amy Tangerine/YouTube; 13TR © Andrea Russett/YouTube; 51BR © AndreasChoice/YouTube; 171BR © ANDREW HUANG/YouTube; 11TR © Aspyn Ovard/YouTube; 95BR; 99TR © Backpacking Bananas/YouTube; 99BR © BACKPACKING BRITS/YouTube; 123BR © Bad Lip Reading/YouTube; 117TR © Bart Baker/YouTube; 17 CR, 50TR, 155BR; 157BR © Bethany Mota/YouTube; 69BR, 157TR © BFvsGF/YouTube; 158TR © blogilates/YouTube; 133TR © Bookables/YouTube; 140TR © Books Beauty Ameriie/YouTube; 131BR © booksandquills/YouTube; 33TR © Bossa Studios/YouTube; 97BR © Brooke Saward/YouTube; 152TR © Brooklyn and Bailey/YouTube; 43BR © bubzbeauty/YouTube; 30BR © CaptainSpraklez/YouTube; 41BR © Carli Bybel/YouTube; 46BR © Caroline Hirons/YouTube; 101TR © CaseyNeistat/YouTube; 70TR, 123TR, 156BR © Caspar/YouTube; 25BR © Chris Stuckmann/YouTube; 33BR © Clash Gaming/YouTube; 44TR © Claudia Sulewski/YouTube; 151BR © Clean & Delicious/YouTube; 80TR © CloeCouture/YouTube; 43TR © clothesencounters/YouTube; 125TR © Comedy Time/YouTube; 153TR © Cooking with Dog/YouTube; 154BR © CrazyRussianHacker/YouTube; 86BR © CreationsToInspire/YouTube; 77TR © Cute Life Hacks/YouTube; 46TR © cutepolish/YouTube; 23TR, 34TR © DanAndPhilGAMES/YouTube; 62BR, 119TR © Daniel Howell/YouTube; 115TR © Danny Duncan/YouTube; 161TR © David Seymour/YouTube; 35TR © DidYouKnowGaming?/YouTube; 78TR © DIYlover/YouTube; 168TR, 174TR ©doddleoddle/YouTube; 125BR © Dog Shirt/YouTube; 149TR © Donal Skehan/YouTube; 53CR © dope2111/YouTube; 28BR © EA SPORTS FIFA/YouTube; 170TR © Ed Sheeran/YouTube; 12BR © Emily Canham; 172BR © EmmaMcGann/YouTube; 154TR © EvanTubeHD/YouTube; 176TR © FBE/YouTube; 160BR © Feast Of Fiction/YouTube; 12TR © Fleur DeForce/YouTube; 95TR, 10TR © FunForLouis/YouTube; 118TR © FunniestClipsTV/YouTube; 8BR © Gabriella/YouTube; 32BR © GameGrumps/YouTube; 29TR © Geek Remix/YouTube; 50BR © Glam&Gore/YouTube; 159BR © Good Mythical Morning/YouTube; 53TR © grav3yardgirl/YouTube; 68BR © Guava Juice/YouTube; 133BR © Hailey in Bookland/YouTube; 167BR © Hannah Trigwell/YouTube; 84TR © Heather Rooney/YouTube; 103BR © Hey Nadine/YouTube; 96BR © High On Life/YouTube; 105BR © How 2 Travelers/YouTube; 161CR © How To Cook That/YouTube; 31BR © iHasCupquake/YouTube; 116TR © IISupermwomanII/YouTube; 122TR © IISupermwomanII/YouTube; 84BR © Innova Crafts/YouTube; 47BR © Inthefrow/YouTube; 27TR © jacksepticeye/YouTube; 30TR, 119BR © jacksepticeye/YouTube; 113BR © jacksfilms/YouTube; 104BR © JacksGap/YouTube; 44BR © Jaclyn Hill/YouTube; 65BR © Jake Mitchell/YouTube; 14TR, 82TR © JENerationDIY/YouTube; 114TR © JennaMarbles/YouTube; 139BR © jessethereader/YouTube; 47TR © Jessica Clements/YouTube; 66TR © Jim Chapman/YouTube; 71TR, 81TR © Joey Graceffa/YouTube; 48TR © Jordon Lipscombe/YouTube; 174BR © JPBouvet/YouTube; 87TR © K Werner Design/YouTube; 78BR © Katherine Elizabeth/YouTube; 52TR © KathleenLights/YouTube; 178BR © KatyPerryVEVO/YouTube; 136TR, 142TR © Katytastic/YouTube; 155TR © kawaiisweetworld/YouTube; 124BR © KickThePj/YouTube; 13BR © Klossy/YouTube; 98BR © Kristen Sarah/YouTube; 167TR © Kurt Hugo Schneider/YouTube; 150TR © Laura in the Kitchen/YouTube; 77BR, 85TR, 160TR © LaurDIY/YouTube; 42TR © Lauren Curtis/YouTube; 89BR © Lily Pebbles/YouTube; 170BR © lindseyrem/YouTube; 137BR © Little Book Owl/YouTube; 156TR © Liv's Healthy Life/

YouTube; 14BR © Maddi Bragg/YouTube; 79TR © Mademoiselle Ruta/YouTube; 106TR © MakeUpByCamila2/YouTube; 116BR © MamaMiaMakeup/YouTube; 10BR © Marcus Butler/YouTube; 100TR © Mari Johnson/YouTube; 7TR © Mark Ferris/YouTube; 81BR © markcrilley/YouTube; 26BR, 31TR, 61BR, 120BR © Markiplier/YouTube; 51TR, 103TR © Marzia/YouTube; 143TR © MatthewSantoro/YouTube; 82BR © MayBaby/YouTube; 5TR, 17TR © Meredith Foster/YouTube; 169BR © Milica Begecki/YouTube; 67TR, 169TR © Miranda Sings/YouTube; 9TR © MissRemiAshten/YouTube; 117BR © MisterEpicMann2/YouTube; 16TR © MoreZoella/YouTube; 97TR © Mr Ben Brown/YouTube; 53BR © MsRosieBea/YouTube; 10TR © MyLifeAsEva/YouTube; 179TR © Nanalew/YouTube; 45TR © Nastazsa/YouTube; 143BR © Nerdwriter1/YouTube; 115BR © nigahiga/YouTube; 52BR, 66BR © NikkieTutorials/YouTube; 149BR © NikkiPhillippi/YouTube; 151TR © Niomi Smart/YouTube; 168BR © OKGoVEVO/YouTube; 71BR © Oli White/YouTube; 28TR © PeanutButterGamer/YouTube; 131TR © PeruseProject/YouTube; 24BR, 26TR, 124TR © PewDiePie/YouTube; 173BR © PianoKeyz/YouTube; 63BR, 64BR © PointlessBlog/YouTube; 9BR © PointlessBlogVlogs/YouTube; 135TR, 135BR, 139TR © polandbananasBOOKS/YouTube; 159TR © POPSUGARfood/YouTube; 177TR © PROJECT Trio/YouTube; 87BR © PsychoSoprano/YouTube; 96TR © PsychoTraveller/YouTube; 171TR © PTXVlogs/YouTube; 138BR © Puffin Books/YouTube; 122BR © Ray William Johnson/YouTube; 105TR © RayaWasHere/YouTube; 70BR, 83BR © Rclbeauty101/YouTube; 132BR, 134BR © readbyzoe/YouTube; 134TR © Reads and Daydreams/YouTube; 173TR © Rebecca Zamolo/YouTube; 29BR © Red vs. Blue; 118BR © RomanAtwood/YouTube; 23BR © RoosterTeeth/YouTube; 61TR, 158BR, 161BR © Rosanna Pansino/YouTube; 42BR, 48BR © Samantha Maria/YouTube; 86TR © Shameless Maya/YouTube; 176BR © Shawn Mendes/YouTube; 16BR, 104TR © Shay Mitchell/YouTube; 68TR © Shine On Media/YouTube; 69TR © Simply Nailogical/YouTube; 25TR © Sky Does Minecraft/YouTube; 63TR, 83TR © Smosh 2nd Channel/YouTube; 32TR, 113TR © Smosh/YouTube; 88TR, 89TR © SoCraftastic/YouTube; 98TR, 106BR © soniastravels/YouTube; 152BR © SORTEDfood/YouTube; 11BR © Sprinkleofglitter; 15TR, 41TR © Tanya Burr/YouTube; 101BR © Tenani/YouTube; 49BR, 100BR © Tess Christine/YouTube; 59TR, 114BR © ThatcherJoe/YouTube; 5BR, 6BR © The Anna Edit/YouTube; 27BR © The Know/YouTube; 142BR © The Lizze Bennet Diaries/YouTube; 179BR © The Music Lab/YouTube; 137TR © TheBookTuber/YouTube; 125CR © TheCatsPyjaaaamas/YouTube; 24TR © theRadBrad/YouTube; 35BR © TheSyndicateProject/YouTube; 141BR © Thoughts on Tomes/YouTube; 65TR © TiffyQuake/YouTube; 120TR © TomSka/YouTube; 153BR © Tonic/YouTube; 175TR, 177BR © Troye Sivan/YouTube; 62TR, 67BR, 121TR, 172TR, 178TR © Tyler Oakley/YouTube; 102BR © vagabrothers/YouTube; 107TR © Video Influencers/YouTube; 136BR © vlogbrothers/YouTube; 138TR © vlogbrothers/YouTube; 141TR © Vsauce/YouTube; 59BR ©Wassabi VLOGS/YouTube; 34BR © WatchMojo.com/YouTube; 49TR © Wayne Goss/YouTube; 175BR © Weirdly Musical/YouTube; 7BR, 80BR © Wengie/YouTube; 85BR © WhatsUpMoms/YouTube; 79BR © withwendy/YouTube; 6TR, 15BR, 60TR, 60BR, 121BR © Zoella/YouTube.

All other images courtesy of Shutterstock.com.

Studio Press and wetheunicorns.com would like to thank the following people:

Michaela Walters, Megan Wastell, Steve Wilson-Beales, Hollie Brooks, Liam Dryden, Benedict Townsend, Charleyy Hodson and Harriet Paul.